IMAGES
of America

ISLAMORADA

IMAGES
of America

ISLAMORADA

Brad Bertelli and Jerry Wilkinson

ARCADIA
PUBLISHING

Published by Arcadia Publishing
Charleston, South Carolina

Library of Congress Control Number: 2013947597

For all general information, please contact Arcadia Publishing:
Telephone 843-853-2070
Fax 843-853-0044
E-mail sales@arcadiapublishing.com
For customer service and orders:
Toll-Free 1-888-313-2665

Visit us on the Internet at www.arcadiapublishing.com

*This book is dedicated to those who have lived these stories as
well as those interested in a glimpse into Islamorada's past.*

CONTENTS

ACKNOWLEDGMENTS

This book would not have been possible without the support of the Historical Preservation Society of the Upper Keys and its two fearless leaders, Jerry and Mary Lou Wilkinson. Thank you to Tom Hambright, historian extraordinaire of the Key West Branch of the Monroe County Library, as well as the families of the Upper Keys who have been so generous over the years with not only their photographs, but with their stories. A special thank-you to Loralea Carrera, Carol Ross, Scott DeWolfe, Rich Russell, and Laura Albritton. As always, thank you to my family and my wife, Michelle. Her love and patience makes my work possible. Thank you, too, to fan number three. Unless otherwise noted, all images reproduced in this book come from the Jerry Wilkinson Collection.

INTRODUCTION

Three bodies of water surround Islamorada: the Atlantic Ocean, the Florida Bay, and the Gulf of Mexico. The intoxicating mix has attracted presidents, movie stars, first-rate characters, and bona fide rapscallions. While the turquoise waters and coral reefs off of Islamorada provide world-class snorkeling and diving, the islands have historically been a beacon for fishermen.

Islamorada is not a single destination, but a collection of islands in the Upper Keys that includes Plantation, Windley, Upper Matecumbe, and Lower Matecumbe Keys, as well as two islands that have been designated as state parks, Indian Key and Lignumvitae Key. However, Islamorada has not always covered so much territory. The original Islamorada townsite was a 15-acre area of Upper Matecumbe Key. No matter the size, what has always been true about Islamorada is that the elements of sky, sun, and water create the desire to slow down and breathe in the coconut-scented breezes.

Islamorada stretches from the northern tip of Plantation Key near mile marker 91 to the southern tip of Lower Matecumbe Key, near mile marker 74. The islands themselves take up approximately 6.4 square miles of space. It was not until December 31, 1997, that Islamorada was incorporated into a Village of Islands. In 2010, Islamorada's population numbered around 6,100.

The chamber of commerce claims Islamorada is the Sport Fishing Capital of the World. The fishing is world-class, with more world-record fish caught in the surrounding waters than anywhere else. Of course, locals have a somewhat different point of view, perhaps best summarized by T-shirts sold at a local watering hole once favored by baseball icon Ted Williams. The shirts proclaim Islamorada as a "quaint little drinking village with a fishing problem."

Fittingly enough, Islamorada is the birthplace of what just might be the quintessential Florida Keys cocktail, the rumrunner. Back in the 1980s, a bartender working at a tiki bar on Windley Key was the first to concoct the frozen blend of rums, lime, and banana and blackberry liqueurs. Rumrunners are an excellent way to combat the subtropical environment and the perfect drink to toast one of the blissfully serene Islamorada sunsets.

That is not to say that the only things Islamorada has to offer are fishing and rum drinks. These islands are home to some pretty cool history. For instance, the ghost town found on Indian Key was once home to the second-largest community in the Keys outside of Key West.

Indian Key was not only a thriving wrecking village and home to one of Florida's first-rate rapscallions, John Jacob Housman. It also had a hotel, bar, and bowling alley. In fact, when James J. Audubon visited the island in 1832 to study the local birds, he complained about the loud parties being thrown.

The community of Indian Key was destroyed by an Indian attack in 1840, but the subsequent slaughter and torching of the island is just one of the notable events that have shaped Islamorada's colorful past. It was a decade or so after the Indian Key massacre destroyed the area's first real community that another began to develop. The community, referred to simply as Matecumbe, began to grow on Upper Matecumbe Key.

One of the first to settle in Matecumbe was Richard H. Russell and his wife, Mary Ann. The Russell family had left the Bahamas in 1838 bound for Key West, where they initially settled. They then moved to the Middle Keys, to Vaca Key, for a while, before packing up again and moving to the northern end of Upper Matecumbe sometime between 1850 and 1855.

The Russells are among a handful of homesteaders who helped to found the Matecumbe community. The Pinders are another. According to the 1870 census, Richard Pinder and his wife, Sarah, were residents of Indian Key, where they farmed bananas. However, by the time the 1880 census rolled around, the Pinders had packed up, left Indian Key, and joined the Russells on nearby Upper Matecumbe. It was the Russells and Pinders who helped to establish the first church and school on the island.

The third major family to join the Russells and Pinders was the Parker family. William Henry Parker and his wife, Amy, first relocated from Eleuthera, Bahamas, to Plantation Key, a couple of islands north of Matecumbe, before later settling on Upper Matecumbe. Since they settled farther south along the beach than the Russell and Pinder families, the latter families did the neighborly thing and moved the church and the school a little farther south so that the structure was conveniently located for all three families.

To move the wooden building, they somehow lodged it between two boats, transported it south, and then dragged it up on the beach at what would be considered the Cheeca Lodge property today. The general location of the church building is still marked by a small graveyard.

A handful of years after the turn of the 20th century, the community known as Matecumbe gradually began to dissipate. It was not that the people went away. There are Russells, Pinders, and Parkers living in the area still. Rather, the name itself, Matecumbe, fell into disuse as a direct result of the actions of one of Henry Flagler's men, William J. Krome.

Krome had been hired by Flagler to survey the impending railroad's right-of-way and was the head engineer responsible for mapping out the route ultimately taken by the Oversea Railway. Work introduced Krome to Upper Matecumbe and, in turn, Krome was introduced to John H. and James W. Russell, the two youngest sons of Richard Russell. The Russells sold Krome 15 acres of Upper Matecumbe land in 1907.

Krome surveyed his property, built a house, and divided his land into 22 lots. It was the thing he did next, however, that left the biggest impression. Krome registered his lots as the town site of Isla Morada. A faded newspaper clipping dated May 7, 1907, reads: "On the north end of Upper Matecumbe Key a new town known as Isla Morada has sprung into existence. . . . It is believed that Isla Morada will become an important tourist stopping place in winter as the location is beautiful and the fishing convenient and excellent."

As the community grew, it adopted the name *Islamorada*, or *Isla Morada*, as it was originally intended. Post Office Islamorada was established in 1908, as was the Islamorada Depot, providing telegraph service, railway express, and a waiting room. Probably no two events have altered the history of these islands more than the coming of Henry Flagler's train and the Great Labor Day Hurricane of 1935. When the eye of the Category 5 hurricane passed over the Islamorada area, it registered as the most powerful storm to ever strike North America.

Spend a little bit of time in Islamorada, and different accounts of the derivation of the place-name will become topics of conversation. The word is Spanish in nature. *Isla* means "island." *Morada*, on the other hand, is a little trickier. When used as an adjective, *morado* means "purple," which explains why some have translated Islamorada to mean Purple Isles. While a colorful story, the islands were not named for the beautifully delicate rice-paper petals of the bougainvillea or the violet-colored sea snails, *Janthina janthina*, professed to have once carpeted the islands' shores.

When used as a feminine noun, morada translates to "abode" or "home," as Krome intended. The matter is explained in a letter written on May 10, 1965, by Mrs. William J. Krome, Isabelle, to her friend, Mal Flanders. Isabelle wrote, "I was not a member of the family at that time and had no part in the selecting of the name, but Mr. Krome told me that it was derived from the Spanish *isla* and *morada*, meaning home." Welcome to Islamorada.

One

LANDMARKS

Islamorada is a fisherman's paradise, with more world-record fish caught in its surrounding waters than anywhere else in the world. With three bodies of water to fish in—the Atlantic Ocean, Florida Bay, and the Gulf of Mexico to the south—the chamber of commerce claims this as the Sport Fishing Capital of the World. Islamorada also claims to be home to the world's largest fishing fleet per square mile.

Marathon's Richard Blaze is responsible for the big lobster, an anatomically correct sculptured crustacean 30 feet high and 40 feet long. Betsy, as the lobster is locally known, took five years to create. Finished in the 1980s, Betsy was originally purchased by Tom Vellanti, owner of the castle-like structure formerly known as the Treasure Village Shopping Center. The lobster has since migrated to the other side of the road.

Islamorada's answer to Sea World is Theater of the Sea. In fact, the marine mammal facility is the second oldest in the United States. Milton Santini, the man who caught and trained Flipper (her real name was Mitzi), supplied the park with some of its first bottle-nosed dolphins. Along with Betsy the giant lobster, the giant queen conch statue outside of Theater of the Sea provides a popular photographic background.

One visit to Windley Key Fossilized Coral Reef State Park is all it takes to reveal the true nature of the Florida Keys. Once upon a time, the islands of the Florida Keys were not only submerged, but part of a living coral reef system. The man pointing his finger in this 1996 photograph is local history guru and author Jerry Wilkinson. He is likely talking about the channeling machine he is standing beside. The machine was used to quarry limestone as well as to create Keystone, a decorative rock created by thinly slicing sections of bedrock and polishing it to a sheen. The small sign dangling from the channeling machine reads "Historical Preservation Society." Wilkinson is the long-standing president of the society. The site opened as a state park in 1999.

The unofficial drink of Islamorada has to be the rumrunner. The frozen concoction, a blend of rum, lime juice, sugar, and banana and blackberry liqueurs, was first concocted on Windley Key. John Egert, aka "Tiki John," invented the subtropical libation while tending bar at the island resort called Holiday Isle in the mid-1970s. One day, Tiki John ran out of sugar and substituted grenadine, which is why the drink is red.

The big mermaid found along the Overseas Highway at mile marker 82 locates the Lor-e-lei Restaurant and Cabana Bar, where backcountry fishing guides and fishermen have gathered to exchange the day's fish tales for decades. This was one of baseball icon Ted Williams's favorite hangouts. Today, it is not only a watering hole, but an excellent locale to watch the sunset and listen to some guitar strumming.

The reason tarpon gather in such numbers beneath the docks at Robbie's Marina can be attributed to Robbie Reckwerdt. Shortly after leasing the property in 1978, Reckwerdt noticed a tarpon floating in the shallows. The injured fish's lower jaw was nearly hanging off. Reckwerdt netted the tarpon and placed it inside an oxygen-rich shrimp tank where he kept bait he sold to fishermen. A local doctor responded with a mattress, needles, and twine, and, after they flopped the fish from the tank to the mattress, the doctor proceeded to sew the fish's jaw back into place. The doctor charged $3 for the house call, and the operation was successful. For six months, Scarface, as the tarpon was nicknamed, recuperated inside the shrimp tank. The tarpon outgrew the tank and was released. However, Scarface never traveled far and routinely showed up looking for handouts. Before long, more and more tarpon began to gather. Today Robbie's is one of Islamorada's bona-fide roadside attractions.

The rhinoceros standing along the Overseas Highway at mile marker 73.8 seemingly guards the sign to the Lower Matecumbe drinking establishment the Safari Lounge, where "the extinct meet to drink." Among locals, the bar is not referred to as the Safari Lounge, but the Dead Animal Bar, or the D.A.B. Animal heads adorn the walls, and the bathroom doors are marked "Tarzan" and "Jane."

When crossing the Channel 2 Bridge that links Lower Matecumbe to Craig Key, visible to the west at approximately mile marker 73.1 are eight coffin-like structures in the water. The concrete forms are bridge piers built for an automobile bridge that was supposed to link Lower Matecumbe to Fiesta Key. Plans for the bridge were washed away during the Great Labor Day Hurricane of 1935.

14

Two

Indian Key,
Lignumvitae Key,
Tea Table Key

The two-masted US schooner *Alligator* was 85 feet long and armed with a dozen cannons. The ship's mission was to fight piracy, as depicted in this image. In 1823, it was escorting a small fleet of vessels liberated from a band of pirates near Guajba, Cuba, back to Charleston, South Carolina. The ship struck the Florida Reef less than four miles from the coast of Upper Matecumbe Key.

A WRECKER OF THE REEF.

Wreckers went into action when a ship crashed on the Florida Reef. They had three primary jobs: save the people, save the cargo, save the ship. Wrecking was pure capitalism; the harder a crew worked, the more they salvaged and the more they earned. Wreckers were paid approximately 25 percent of the goods salvaged during an operation. This included the value of the vessel, should it be saved.

It paid to be the first licensed wrecking captain to arrive at the site of a wrecked ship. Wrecking captains pushed their crews to brave stormy, even dangerous weather. The first captain on site, should the skipper of the ship in peril request assistance, became the designated wreck master. He alone determined how the operation would be conducted. He also received the largest slice of the salvage award.

WRECKERS AT WORK.

In 1837, the *Charleston Courier* published a story by Dr. Benjamin B. Strobel (pictured), a physician and writer who had traveled extensively through the Keys. "From all that I heard of wreckers," he wrote, "I expected to see a parcel of low, dirty pirate looking crafts, officiated and manned by a set of black whiskered fellows, who carried murder in their very looks." Contrarily, wreckers were a floundering vessel's salvation. Dr. Strobel continued, "I was, however, very agreeably surprised to find their vessels fine large sloops and schooners, regular clippers, kept in first rate order, and that the Captains were jovial, good humored sons of Neptune, who manifested every disposition to be polite and hospitable, and to afford every facility to persons passing up and down the Reef. The crews were composed of hearty, well dressed, honest looking men."

Indian Key used to be called Matanza, Spanish for "Slaughter Key," after an alleged, and undocumented, massacre of 400 stranded French sailors. There was, however, an Indian attack in the island's history. The 11-acre island in the Atlantic shallows just off the coast of Upper Matecumbe was called Cayo Comfort by Bahamian sailors. The island is at a roughly midway point along the Florida Reef. It boasts a reputation for remaining relatively mosquito-free. Freshwater springs could once be found on Lower Matecumbe. One of the first times the place-name *Indian Key* appeared was on Bernard Roman's 1775 chart. After Florida became a US territory in 1821, Indian Key became a community of wreckers, turtlers, and fishermen. Silas Fletcher became the first white settler. He arrived on the island in 1824 and built the first general store.

INDIAN KEY, THE WRECKERS' RENDEZVOUS.

John Jacob Housman is credited with transforming Indian Key into a wrecking community. He arrived in 1830, bought the general store, and began to develop the island. A street system was created and wharves were built, along with shops for blacksmiths, carpenters, and sail makers. The island was also home to a nine-pin bowling alley, bar, and hotel. Housman spent a reported $40,000 landscaping the island with tropical plants, fruits, and vegetables.

Shown here is the Staten Island, New York, home of the man who grew up to become the wrecker king of Indian Key. That man, John Jacob Housman, was born in 1799. One of nine children, he was the son of an oysterman. During the Second Seminole War, Housman organized Company B, 10th Regiment, Florida Militia to guard Indian Key. All able-bodied men between 18 and 45 were enlisted.

Henry Edward Perrine was born on April 5, 1797, in Cranbury, New Jersey. Perrine graduated from medical school in 1819, but he is not remembered for his love of medicine. Perrine moved to Indian Key on Christmas Day 1838 and began developing the Tropical Plant Company. His goal was to make South Florida the most productive tropical plant center in the United States. His children are pictured here from left to right: Sarah, Henry Jr., and Hester Perrine.

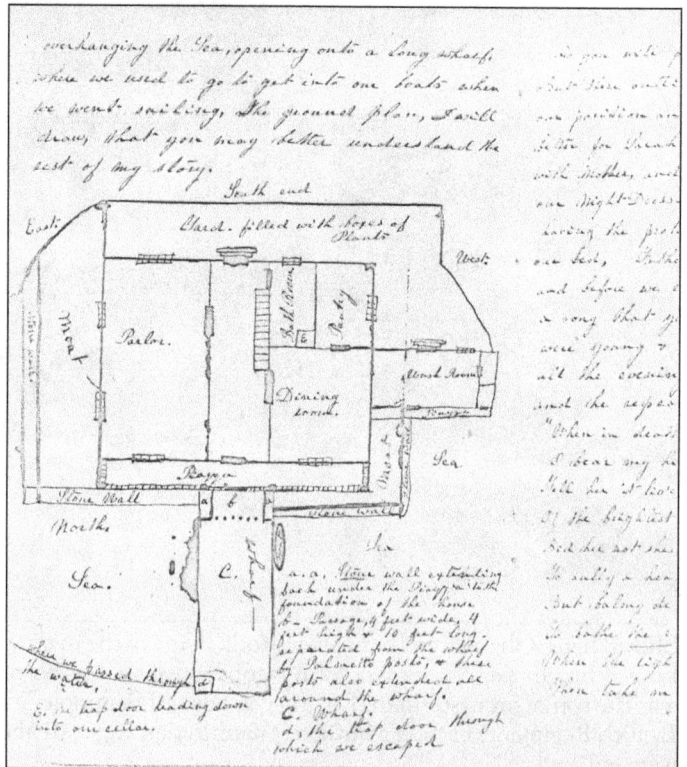

This diagram of the Perrine house on Indian Key was taken from the pages of Hester Perrine's diary. The sketch of the first floor reveals a parlor, dining room, pantry, bathroom, and washroom. Outside, a stone wall and moat partially surround the house on three sides. On the fourth side is a yard filled with boxes of plants. Beneath the wharf was a turtle kraal, or live turtle pen.

During the Second Seminole War, Indian Key was both isolated and stocked with supplies. While Housman repeatedly petitioned the government for protection, he was forced to establish his private militia. Housman paid each man 30¢ a day plus a 50¢ credit toward rations. The Navy increased area patrols in 1838, the year Dr. Perrine arrived. He reported 40 buildings on the island. When a fort was established in the area, Housman disbanded the Florida patrol. Lt. John McLaughlin took command of area operations and decided to withdraw nearly every soldier from the area and launch an offensive into the Everglades to root out the Indian scourge. By August 6, 1840, McLaughlin and his men left the area. At 2:00 a.m. on August 7, Chief Chekika and his band of braves paddled up, attacked, and nearly burned down the island.

Born in Baltimore in 1812, John Thomas McLaughlin was a career Navy man who "received a ball to his breast" during an Indian attack on Fort Monroe in 1837. Commissioned a lieutenant in 1838 and given command of a small fleet, McLaughlin used Indian Key as a Naval station and hospital. A yellow fever outbreak prompted his move to nearby Tea Table Key in 1839. He was investigated for misusing resources.

After Indian Key was destroyed in the attack, Housman and his wife went to Key West, where he found work on a wrecker's crew. Historians agree that he was crushed to death between the hulls of two ships, but not where he was ultimately buried, even if the inscription on this tombstone found on the island reads "John Jacob Housman." A replica of the marker has been placed on the island.

Husband and wife Terry J. and Ann Starck were walking along the shore of Indian Key in the 1960s when they noticed the top of a human skull sticking out of the ground. They excavated what turned out to be a grave and reported finding a complete skeleton. Fragments of wood and some metal pieces were inside the grave, and the skeleton was buried only a few inches beneath the surface. They covered up the skeleton before they left. Several weeks later, the couple returned to the island and found the grave had again been excavated, but this time the skeleton had been removed. The only thing left behind were several teeth. Terry took some of the teeth and placed them in his pocket; unfortunately, when leaving the island, the Starcks were caught in a severe squall, Terry's pocket ripped, and the teeth fell into the water. This photograph was taken on their first trip.

Completed in 1873, Alligator Lighthouse cost $185,000 to build. The iron was forged by Paulding Kemble of Cold Springs, New York, and shipped in parts to Indian Key. Out at the reef, iron supports were driven 10 feet into the coral by a 2,000-pound hammer, one inch at a time. The 136-foot-tall structure stands about three and a half miles offshore. The name is derived from the wreck of the US schooner *Alligator*, which struck the reef in 1823. Despite all efforts, the pirate-hunting warship could not be dislodged from the corals. The ship was cleared of tackle, weapons, and cargo, and then blown to smithereens, as there was no sense in leaving anything for pirates to scavenge. The only remains are ballast stones in 10 feet of water east of the lighthouse.

The island west of the Lignumvitae Channel Bridge was first called Cayo de las Lena, "Firewood Key." Documentation suggests the Spanish used the island as a respite for their sailors; evidence of kitchen middens and a burial ground indicate Indians were the earliest inhabitants. A 1765 British map declares it Jenkinson Island. It was not until 1772 that the words "Lignum Vitae Key" showed up on nautical charts. The 280-acre island is unique to the archipelago not only for its elevation (a whopping 16 feet above sea level), but also for its virgin natural hardwood hammock. The timber on the island was never harvested or burned. The diary of William Hackley, a Key West lawyer, indicates that he visited the island in 1831. He wrote about a Captain Rooke who was clearing land to build a house.

Dr. J.B. Holder's account of his trip through the islands in the 1860s described a large Norwegian sailor by the name of Captain Cole living there. The story appeared in an 1871 edition of *Harper's New Monthly* magazine, in a piece titled "Along the Florida Reef." Cole was said to have been an educated man with a collection of books written in a handful of languages. Like Captain Housman before him, Cole cultivated watermelons, which he then sold in Key West. Next came Capt. William H. Bethel, a resident of Indian Key who managed a small sisal plantation here. It was hoped that sisal fiber could compete with the hemp trade, but fruits and vegetables proved a better commodity. Bethel bought the island for a reported 75¢ per acre; he became the first legal owner of Lignumvitae Key.

Lignumvitae Key was sold to brothers Thomas A. and Edward A. Hine in 1881 for $2,000. Ditching sisal, pineapples, and watermelons, they invested in coconuts. The island was then sold to William John Matheson of the Biscayne Chemical Company in 1919. Matheson was the president and had been overseeing coconut plantations on Key Biscayne as well as at least two other farms on Upper Matecumbe Key. Since the island's purchase by Matheson, it has known a handful of "managers" who kept watch over the island for its absentee landlords. Charlotte and Russell Neidhauk arrived in 1954. The state assumed control of the island in 1971, and in 1972, the island was declared Lignumvitae Key Botanical State Park. Ranger-guided tours are available twice daily, at 10:00 a.m. and 2:00 p.m., Thursday through Monday.

Matheson's authorized alterations to the island included construction of a two-story, four-bedroom house that still stands today. In addition, three acres surrounding the house were cleared, and six cannons were salvaged from the HMS *Winchester*, which struck Carysfort Reef in 1695 and sank. The 87-foot windmill was erected to provide electricity, a cistern was created, and an airstrip was cleared on the west end of the island.

Exotic animals were introduced to the island, including Mexican burros, Angora goats from India, and giant Galapagos tortoises. The goats were quickly shipped back because they were butting their heads against the shallow-rooted indigenous trees and uprooting them. Because the tortoises preferred the exotic succulents to the native cactus they were brought in to feed on, the turtles were carted off to the Crandon Park Zoo.

Shown here are Russell and Charlotte Niedhauk. Russ was born in the Pennsylvania Dutch country, and Charlotte was of French origins. Russell was the apprentice to a master mechanic at a steel mill before moving to Florida in 1928. Landing in Fort Lauderdale, he found work sailing a yacht for the Baldwin Locomotive Works. Russell married Charlotte, and the two served as caretakers on Elliot Key in 1934 and 1935, where they weathered the Great Labor Day Hurricane. Her book, *Charlotte's Story*, details her early adventures island-watching and details her experience. Russ and Charlotte were hired as caretakers on Lignumvitae Key in 1954 after three "Miamians" bought the island for $125,000 the year before. Dr. Nelson Pearson was a physician, J. Abney Cox was a potato farmer; each owned a quarter share. Dr. E.C. Lunsford, a dentist, owned the lion's share of the island.

Lignumvitae Key has no road and no place to drive to. The vast majority of the island is home to a lush subtropical hammock. Still, Russell Niedhauk decided he wanted to bring his car over to the island. With no ferry system operating in the area, he had to improvise. With the help of friends, he managed to load the automobile on two separate skiffs and use them like pontoons.

The Niedhauks spent over two decades as caretakers of Lignumvitae Key. The state took possession of the island, as well as Indian Key, in 1970. Both islands were established as state parks the following year. After a misunderstanding took place between the state and the Niedhauks, Russ and Charlotte gave up their island post. They resigned as caretakers in 1978 and moved aboard their houseboat, the *Nepenthe*, pictured here.

Three

MATECUMBE

This image of Upper Matecumbe is dated March 1906. Tea Table is prominent in the background, while off in the distance, Indian Key is visible. Judging by the proximity of the two islands in the distance, this site is likely in the mile marker 80–81 area, near the current location of Hampton Inn and Lazy Days Restaurant.

This 1906 photograph shows Tea Table Key. George Gauld noted, "The small key off the west end of New Matecumbe has a remarkable single tree at the south end of it like an umbrella." On his 1775 map, the 3.11-acre islet is called Umbrella Kay. Before the Second Seminole War, the island was used as farmland by Indian Key resident Lemil Otis. During that war, the island was claimed by the Navy, structures were built, including a hospital ward, and the island was declared Fort Paulding. A causeway linking the island to the highway was built sometime before 1970. Today, it is Terra's Key, named for the current owner, James Terra. The five-bedroom, six-bath house is a gated escape with two swimming pools and a private tennis court, available for around $10,000 a week.

Three groups are considered founding Matecumbe families: the Russells, the Pinders, and the Parkers. Each settled on the Upper Matecumbe beach to take advantage of ocean breezes that cooled their houses and provided a modicum of pest control. The community at large was known as Matecumbe; family compounds adopted identifiers like Russellville, Pinderville, and Parkerville. The small building on the right of this Pinderville house is the grocery store.

Before Henry Flagler brought his train, families relied on boats to communicate with the outside world as well as for the transportation of goods and people. Because of the shallow nature of the water surrounding these islands, long piers were built to accommodate vessels with deeper drafts. In addition to the two skiffs that can be seen tied up to the pier, there is a third vessel, from which this photograph was taken.

Churches in the Upper Keys in the early communities of Planter and Matecumbe began to be written about in 1881. Richard Pinder initiated construction of this one-room building in 1894 for the Matecumbe Methodist congregation. The building was originally erected to serve the Russell and Pinder families and was initially located north of where the Cheeca Lodge property stands today. In 1894, the Parker family settled on Upper Matecumbe, south of Russellville and Pinderville. In 1897, the church was moved to accommodate the Parkers by strategically placing it between two boats and transporting it south via the ocean. The wooden structure was unloaded and moved onto the beach at what would now be considered Cheeca Lodge property. This image was captured in 1906 by a photographer associated with Henry Flagler's crew.

In 1870, Richard and Sarah Pinder were farming bananas on Indian Key. They later moved and became the second of the three founding families to settle on Upper Matecumbe. This is their grandson, Preston Pinder. He was acting foreman during construction of the Matecumbe Methodist church, where he was a member for 50 years. He also served as a pastor. Preston Pinder was also a fishing guide at the Matecumbe Club.

William J. Krome, hired by Flagler to survey the impending railroad's right-of-way, was the head engineer responsible for mapping out the route ultimately taken by the Oversea Railway. Work introduced Krome to Upper Matecumbe and, in turn, Krome was introduced to John H. and James W. Russell, the two youngest sons of Richard Russell. Krome purchased 15 acres of Upper Matecumbe land from the brothers in 1907.

Krome surveyed his property, built a house, and divided his land into 22 lots. William J. Krome officially registered the locale as the townsite of Isla Morada. Some years later, Krome's wife would write a letter to her friend, Mal Flanders, explaining that the Spanish derivation of Islamorada was *Isla*, meaning "island," and *Morada*, meaning "home." The house on the left is Krome's; the other belonged to P.L. Wilson.

The Oversea Railway connected to its southernmost terminal in 1912, but it began servicing the Upper Keys years before. By 1908, train service reached south to Knights Key dock, stretching over a mile out into Moser Channel. The railroad altered the flow of commerce, away from the ocean. As a result, community centers shifted from the boat docks and piers at the shoreline and toward the train tracks.

In the January 6, 1912, edition of the *Miami News*, under the Islamorada news section, the following was recorded: "Miss Geneva Parker invited a number of young people to her house Sunday night to watch the Old Year out and the New Year in. The hours were passed quickly by singing and talking. About 10:30 delicious refreshments were served. Those present were: Miss Geneva Parker, Miss Edith Jenkens, Jenetta and Bessie Cothron." In this 1913 photograph, Bessie Cothron is the girl on the far right. The other girls are friends visiting from Key West who were attending high school at St. Mary's Convent. Bessie Cothron was the daughter of Reynolds and Mary Cothron. Her brother, Alonzo, took over the family construction business, whose building credits include the Tavernier Hotel.

The townsite of Isla Morada began to coalesce with the establishment of Post Office Islamorada in 1908, the year the Islamorada Depot was established and began providing telegraph service, railway express service, and a waiting room. While initially, Matecumbe and Islamorada referred to the same general community, the place-name Matecumbe seemed to fall out of fashion. The men in this photograph are posing beneath the Islamorada sign. There were two depots of Upper Matecumbe. The northern depot was referred to as Islamorada, while the southern depot was called the Matecumbe Depot. The two doors on the side of the building led to restrooms. Posted above the left-hand door is "White." The door on the right is labeled "Colored."

The coral rock version of the Matecumbe School was built around 1924. The two-room structure was built on land donated by William Matheson, owner of Lignumvitae Key. The building was one of two identical structures built in the Upper Keys, both of which were constructed as school buildings. The other schoolhouse can still be seen on Key Largo at approximately mile marker 98.5. That building, which has undergone some reconstruction, now serves as the Moose lodge. Upper Keys schools provided education up to the eighth grade. According to school board records, both schools were forced to temporarily close in 1924 due to mosquitoes. Prior to the Great Labor Day Hurricane of 1935, classes at the Matecumbe School were taught by Ferran Pinder and Charles "Prof" Albury. The school was washed away in the storm.

The second incarnation of the Matecumbe Methodist Church was located on property donated by William Matheson and built around 1926. The first marriage ceremony performed at the church joined Alonzo Cothron and Florence Pinder on June 9, 1926. Reverend Munro was brought up from Key West to perform the service. The Reverend R.E. and Mrs. Carlson were assigned to the Matecumbe church for a few months prior to Labor Day in 1935. Visible behind the church building is the two-room coral rock schoolhouse. The church was destroyed in the hurricane, and the reverend and his wife died. His body was not found for 10 days. After the storm, Preston Pinder oversaw construction of the new church. That building, once located behind the hurricane monument, has since been donated to the Baptists and moved to mile marker 81.

The Matecumbe Cemetery was the third component of the William Matheson land donation, found today on the Cheeca Lodge property. The hallowed grounds served the Pinders and Parkers; the Russell family cemetery had already been established. Etta Delores Pinder, who died at 15, is buried beneath the angel in this photograph. The statue survived the impact of the killer hurricane nearly intact; it lost part of one wing.

The Highway Gospel Church, pictured here, was a Brethern church built shortly before the Great Labor Day Hurricane. The one-room wood building was erected by Copeland Johnson of Key West. It was located on the southbound side of the Old Highway, facing the Atlantic Ocean. The building was destroyed in the Labor Day hurricane. Copeland Johnson, who had been living with the Russell family, was killed in the storm.

Building SR 4A 1927

News of a plan to construct an automobile road to connect the mainland to the Keys first spread in 1926, when Monroe County officials appropriated $2.5 million for road improvements. Dade County officials agreed to finance 11 miles of road to connect the mainland to its southernmost terminus, Little Card Point. When Tavernier resident Cliff Carpenter drove his new 1928 coupe from Miami to Tavernier, he referred to it as a "bumpy rock road."

This steamroller, seen around 1927, is smoothing out the dirt and rock road that would become the first incarnation of the Oversea Highway. The train depot on the left is the station Matecumbe 1444. By the late 1920s, road systems had been completed that connected Miami to Upper Matecumbe to the north and Key West to No Name Key to the south. The 41-mile gap separating these two points was serviced by an automobile ferry.

In 1927, J. Otto Kirchheiner was the chairman of the Monroe County commissioners. He is credited as being the first person to traverse the highway via automobile, leaving Key West for the mainland on July 18, 1927. The photograph of this motorcade was taken on January 22, 1928. The motorcade had departed from Miami bound for Key West. The highway opened to the public a few days later, on January 25.

The Oversea Railway and the Oversea Highway were both in operation at the same time. The primary difference between the two structures was that, while the train chugged along a continuous route, a 41-mile gap in the road had to be traversed by an automobile ferry. Bridges and roadways paralleled the train tracks. The speed limit on bridges was 10 miles per hour. No stopping was allowed on the approach or bridge.

Completing the drive from Miami to Key West required taking a ferry, like the *Key West*, pictured here. The *Key West* was one of three automobile ferries purchased from Gibb's Shipyard in Jacksonville at a total cost of $850,000. Ferries were used to bridge the 41-mile gap in the highway that separated Lower Matecumbe from No Name Key. It was an unreliable service, as boats were often delayed by low tides and swift currents.

Before completion of the Lower Matecumbe ferry terminal, a temporary ferry landing had been constructed at the tip of Upper Matecumbe. The gas station in the foreground was in the parking lot area of the old Papa Joe's restaurant. The landing is visible in the immediate background, and tracks of the Oversea Railway can be seen in the distance. This undated photograph was likely taken around 1927.

The permanent ferry station, seen here around 1930, was constructed at the southern terminus of Lower Matecumbe. As long as everything was running smoothly, the ferry would take approximately four hours to complete the crossing. The vessel was capable of transporting 20 cars at a time. Vehicles less than 14 feet long were charged $3.50; those longer than 16 feet, $6.50. Ticket prices included the driver. Passengers were charged $1 each.

The ferry departed at 8:00 a.m. and 1:00 p.m. daily. To cater to those waiting, the Terminal Lunch served breakfast and lunch. Besides the ferry landing, only two other permanent structures stood on Lower Matecumbe: the building used by the Crosland Fish Company, headquartered in Miami; and Terminal Lunch, listed in a 1928 brochure advertising local businesses. Veterans Camp No. 3 was constructed directly behind the building.

These two photographs show the Matecumbe Club, built for select members of the New York Cotton Exchange. Wilbur Johnson and Archie Gwathway purchased the beachfront property, and S.W. Eccels constructed the building in 1919. The first floor was used as a lounge area, the second floor had five bedrooms with private bathrooms, and a loft area was used as a large dormitory. The exclusive fishing club was limited to 11 members. Located at the ocean end of Johnson Street, which was named for one of the club's presidents, the club was referred to by some locals as the Millionaire's Club. Bertram Pinder acted as the caretaker for the property for 12 years. The building to the left of the club was used by staff for the purposes of cooking and cleaning.

The Caribbee Colony opened on the ocean side of Upper Matecumbe in 1930. The 12-building resort was developed by George E. Merrick, the man who established the prestigious Miami suburb of Coral Gables. Merrick married Eunice Peacock, the daughter of Coconut Grove pioneers Charles and Isabella Peacock. George and Eunice inherited the Upper Matecumbe property from her parents. George developed a tropical resort equipped with private cottages, a dance hall, a restaurant, and a pier. A four-course dinner at the restaurant, including steak or lobster and a slice of key lime pie or coconut cake, cost $1. The Florida East Coast Railway ran the South Seas Special, which departed Miami Royal Palm Park Station and delivered guests almost directly to Merrick's resort. Note the fine print on the sign: "select your crawfish and stone crabs from our live pens."

The thatched roofs adorning the recreation buildings at the Caribbee Colony were constructed by Seminole Indians hired by Merrick. According to longtime Islamorada resident Leo Johnson, the Indians would not accept a check for payment and demanded to be paid in cash. The Caribbee was one of the early luxury resorts developed in the area. La Siesta Resort at mile marker 80 can be found there now.

George Merrick developed the Caribbee Colony property, but he was not a hands-on owner. J. Wade and Marie Dumas managed the property until 1935. J. Wade is holding the car door open, and it may be Marie seated inside the vehicle. Unfortunately, the writing is too small to read the menu board being held by the waiter.

The Russell Arms Hotel was built by Doddridge and Burnell Russell of Key West and became a popular spot to stay among Islamorada's burgeoning tourist attractions. An announcement posted in the *Miami News*, dated August 11, 1927, reads: "The Russell Arms Hotel, Matecumbe Key, Fl. Home of the Bone-Fish. A modern 27 room hotel built near what is now the temporary terminus of the Oversea Highway. Sand beach bathing—deep sea fishing. Up-to-date dining room service—sea food a specialty. Ideally located for week-end patrons from Miami and Homestead. Summer Rates: $5.50 a day; $33.50 a week." The hotel once stood where MA's Fish Camp stands today.

Capt. Edward "Capt. Ed" Butters and Fern Telva Drey met at an Ohio railroad station, and, two months later, they married. The couple lived in South Dakota before moving to Miami in 1926 with his parents. Ed did construction work on the Miami-Dade Courthouse. Fern surprised Ed with the purchase of a lot on North Key Largo. That lot became home to their entry into the hospitality world. The Key Inn, a hotel and restaurant, featured Fern's cooking. Thomas Edison was a frequent patron. The Butters were managing a growing business, and the hotel suffered damage during a 1929 hurricane. As a result, the Butters sold the Key Inn to Mabel Harris, sister of perennial Florida Keys politician Harry Harris. Seen here in 1928, Fern and Ed stand on the beach with a bag filled with conchs.

After selling the Key Inn, Ed and Fern Butters moved south to Upper Matecumbe, where, in 1931, they purchased the Russell Arms Hotel for $80,000. They continued to serve dignitaries and celebrities, including Presidents Eisenhower and Truman, Thomas Edison, and radio and television personality Arthur Godfrey. For the Butters, the purchase of the Islamorada property was a dream come true. Fern Butters is pictured here holding the car door.

Of the five sites designated Florida East Coast Railway rock quarries, two were located on Windley Key. One quarry was where the state park is today, and the other was across the highway at Theater of the Sea. Flagler's men used the quarries to support the Oversea Railway. After the tracks were completed, it was discovered that the slabs of limestone substrate could be shipped to Miami, sliced thin, polished, and sold for decorative purposes.

Charles Cale Sr. is seen operating the channeling machine at the Windley Key quarry for Mizner Industries. The channeling machine chiseled two narrow crisscross grooves into the fossilized coral bedrock. The machine's chisel was used to cut a small trench in the limestone six inches at a time. After one pass, the machine would make another, cutting the trench six inches deeper every time until a suitably sized slab was created.

Charlie Cale Sr. (right) came to Miami after moving from South Dakota with his father and grandfather in 1899. He settled in the Upper Keys and found work at the Windley Key quarry with the Keystone Rock Company. Cale Sr. married Alice Moore (left), the sister of Lewis Moore, who had moved to the Windley Key area to work at the quarry with the Cales.

The Snake Creek Fishing Lodge offered rooms, meals, shower baths, and deep-sea fishing. It was located on the Snake Creek bank of Windley Key. Lenoy Russell, born around 1896, ran the operation. His wife was named Laura. In 1934, when the Federal Emergency Relief Agency (FERA) began supervision of the project to bridge the 41-mile gap in the Oversea Highway separating Lower Matecumbe from No Name Key, FERA officials leased the building for use as offices and a hospital ward. The fishing lodge was said to have been located just 1,000 feet from the first of three housing camps used by World War I veterans, the workforce sent to the Keys to build the bridges. Workers stationed at the Windley Key camp worked at a quarry on the other side of Snake Creek, on Plantation Key.

Plantation Key and Indian Key were the only two islands in the Upper Keys where large sailing vessels were constructed. An early Plantation Key homesteader was John "Brush" Pinder. The Pinder family compound was said to have been located approximately half a mile north of Little Snake Creek, which used to wind across Plantation Key south of the Rain Barrel property. During construction of the Florida East Coast Railway, Flagler's men filled the creek. In the Prohibition years, the mouth of the Oceanside creek was reportedly a favorite hiding place for rumrunners. This photograph shows Plantation Key residents Raymond Johnson (left) and "Brush" Pinder wearing necklaces of dried sponges. The little girl in the boat is Mary Pinder Ely. Pinder's boat, *Island Home*, can be seen in the distance.

Johnny "Brush" Pinder built the *Island Home*, a 45-ton, 60-foot schooner. The vessel was used to transport goods, crops such as pineapples, people, and mail between Miami and Key West. Built in 1903, the boat was designed by John Watkins of Key West and constructed on Pinder's Plantation Key property. A local Bahamian carpenter, "Old Whiskers" Haskell, provided the workmanship.

William Pinder (left), John William "Brush" Pinder (center), and Raymond Maloney pose with a loggerhead turtle. For the early settlers, turtles were a valuable source of protein. They would be captured alive and kept in pens called turtle kraals. Before freezers and refrigerators became a part of everyday life, the best way to have fresh meat was to keep it alive. Turtle eggs were also harvested.

In 1932, a group of 15,000 veterans marched on Washington. They tried to convince Congress to pass a bill authorizing early remittance of the monies promised to them by the World War I Bonus Law. The law promised every veteran of the war a certificate, a bonus check, eligible for deposit in 1945. President Hoover had the Bonus Marchers, as the vets were called, chased off the streets of Washington with bayonets and tear gas. When President Roosevelt took office, one of his first orders of business was getting America back to work. He enacted the Federal Emergency Relief Administration. One of the work projects undertaken was the building of the solid bridge system to create a continuous road from Miami to Key West. By 1934, hundreds of World War I veterans had been shipped to Islamorada and put to work.

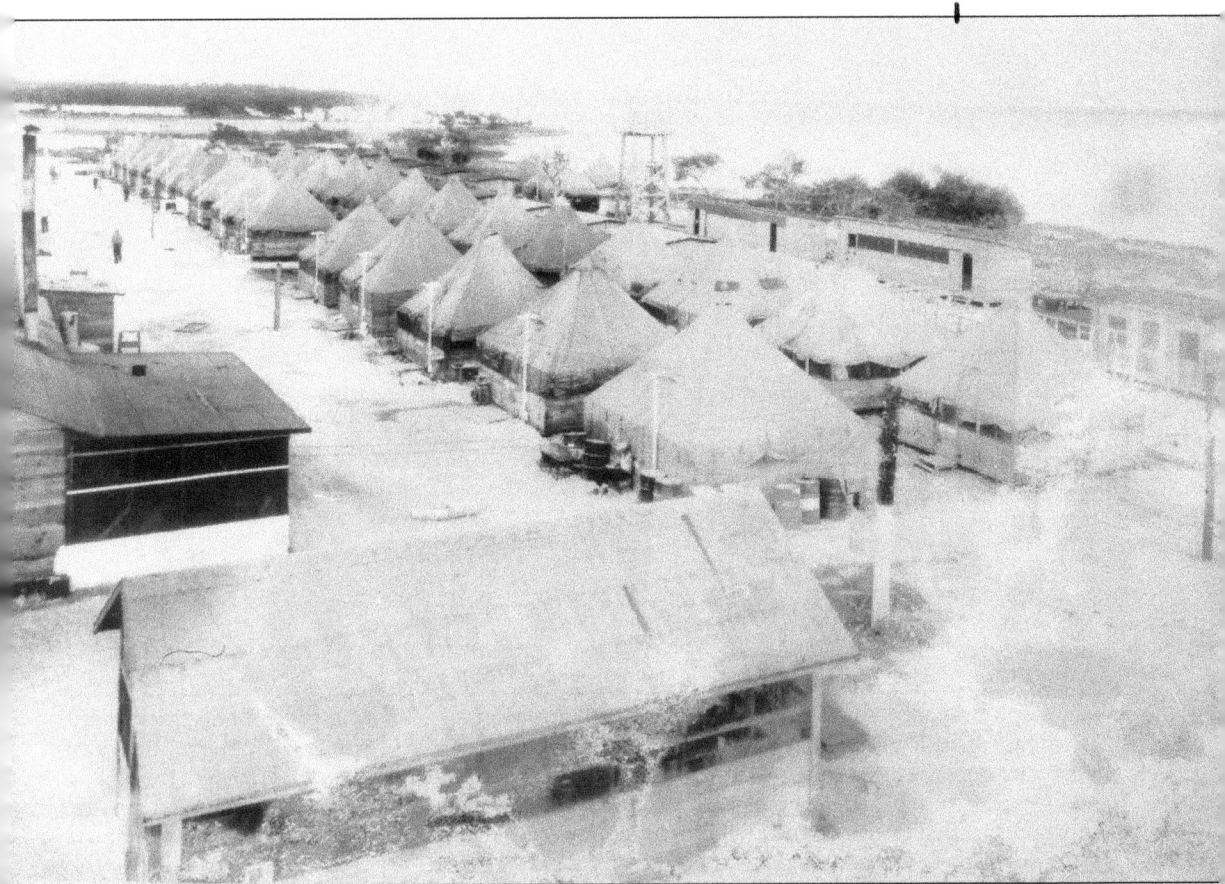

Three work camps were established in Islamorada to house the veteran workforce. Each camp was capable of housing up to 250 workers, with up to eight men assigned to each tent. Camp No. 1 was on Windley Key, just across Snake Creek from Plantation Key. In addition, two camps were created on Lower Matecumbe Key. The vets were primarily used to cut and transport blocks of limestone substrate from the quarry to building sites down the line. The exact locale of the Plantation Key quarry is uncertain. The general area is just north of the entrance to the Venetian Shores neighborhood. This is a photograph taken of Camp No. 1 dated July 20, 1935. Headquarters for the project were set up at the Matecumbe Hotel, which once stood where MA's Fish Camp stands today.

These photographs show the southern tip of Plantation Key, looking south. The tracks used by the Oversea Railway are delineated by the row of power lines strung beside them. Tracks to accommodate the crane (used to load the quarried slabs) were built to parallel Flagler's train. The crane was used to lift the coral blocks onto the train's flatbed car for transportation to Camp No. 3, where the first bridge in the chain, linking Lower Matecumbe to Jewfish Bush Key, was under construction. The quarry rock was being used for two primary purposes: the construction of the bridge system, and for a schoolhouse being developed across the street from the old post office building along De Leon Street.

A rotary trenching machine carved up the Plantation Key quarry, producing both crushed rock fill and rectangular limestone blocks. The blocks were cut out of the island, shipped to Lower Matecumbe, and used as filler for the construction of the first bridge in the system linking Lower Matecumbe and No Name Keys. The first bridge built would link the island to Jewfish Bush Key, called Fiesta Key today.

After the limestone slabs were cut from the Plantation Key quarry, they were transported south to cofferdams being constructed in shallows off Lower Matecumbe Key. The cofferdams were filled with the coral substrate slabs (shown here) taken from the Plantation Key quarry site. The cofferdams were filled with the quarry rock to reduce the amount of concrete needed.

Camp No. 3, the largest of the camps, was located at the southern end of Lower Matecumbe. It was home to a mess tent, barbershop, and recreation hall and was the only camp to have a harbor accessible from the Channel 2 and Channel 5 bridges. The camp operated as a seaport servicing the quarter boat *Sarasota* as well as dredges, barges, tugboats, a floating concrete plant, and a mosquito control boat. Camp No. 3 stored equipment and building materials, and contained 64 cabins used as housing barracks. It was home to both veteran and civilian workers. A point of contention among the vets was that, while eight vets were assigned to their cabins, civilian cabins only housed four men. Camp No. 5, found at the northern end of the island, was used primarily as a housing camp.

One of the vessels using the docking area at Camp No. 3 was the quarter boat *Sarasota*. Ed H. Sheeran, who had worked with Flagler during construction of the railway, became the head engineer for the state road department during construction of the new series of automobile bridges. The *Sarasota* is seen tied to a series of mooring posts. It operated as a sort of "office barge."

The motto of the *Key Veteran News* was, "Published weekly by the veterans rehabilitation camps." This April 20, 1935, edition reports that 30-odd men interested in playing baseball met at the Matecumbe Methodist Church to discuss ways to "firmly establish" the sport for the men in the camps. The cover art, drawn by T.W. Conrad, illustrates an array of "suits" worn by the men.

This photograph, taken on August 17, 1935, shows the intersection of the old State Road 4A and De Leon Avenue. The telephone pole in the background indicates the location of the railroad tracks. Three buildings stand in the foreground. The building at left is the "new" post office. Brothers J.A. and Clifton Russell shared the duties of postmaster and ran the Ocean View Restaurant, also housed in the building. The foundation of that building is still visible. The building at center is what used to be the old post office building. The third building was the grocery store. The Islamorada depot can be seen behind the grocery store.

Four

THE GREAT
LABOR DAY HURRICANE

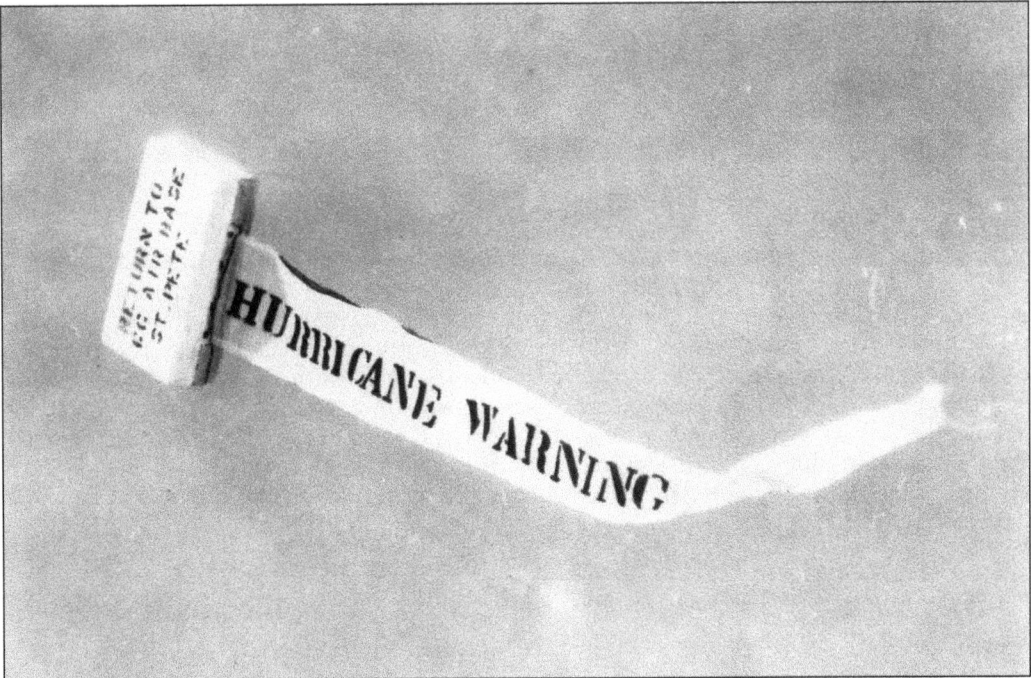

Hurricane warning floats were dropped by Coast Guard aircraft to alert vessels. A message of warning would be contained inside the box to alert captains to adjust their coordinates accordingly. After steering to safety, captains were given the responsibility of returning the box to the appropriate Coast Guard station. In this case, the box was in St. Petersburg. This signal box was dropped to warn of the impending 1935 hurricane.

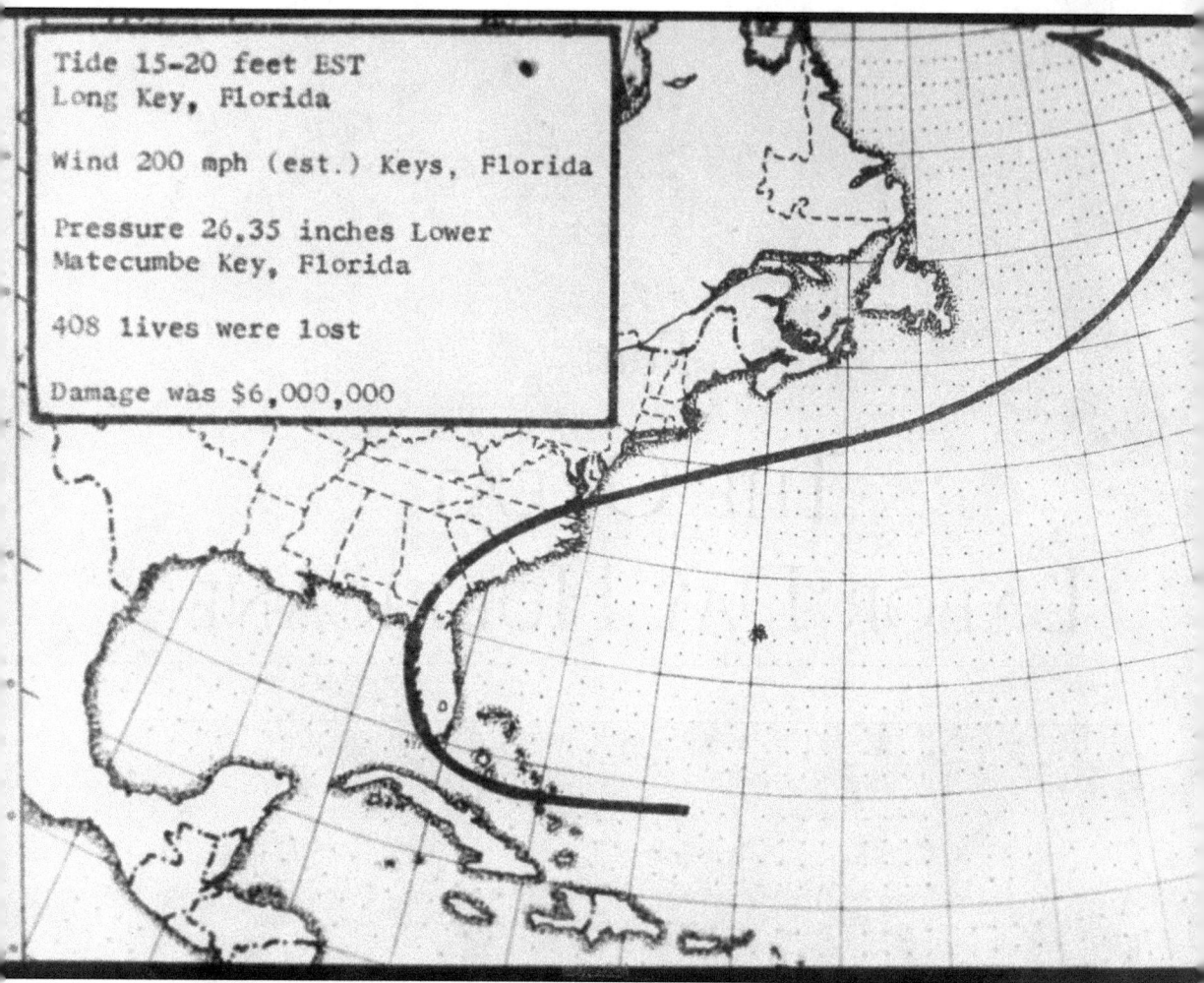

Tide 15-20 feet EST
Long Key, Florida

Wind 200 mph (est.) Keys, Florida

Pressure 26.35 inches Lower
Matecumbe Key, Florida

408 lives were lost

Damage was $6,000,000

A slow-moving weak disturbance of tropical nature formed east of the Bahamas on or around August 28, 1935. It was August 31 before the weather bureau issued its first advisory regarding the storm, referring to it as "a small system of noteworthy strength." The next day, the storm was described by the weather bureau as a tropical disturbance with "shifting gales and probably winds of hurricane force." The eye of the hurricane passed over Lower Matecumbe Key on September 2, Labor Day. The Category 5 storm blew ashore, and was the most powerful hurricane to strike North America to that point. In addition to winds estimated as being in the 200-mile-per-hour range, 17 feet of storm surge washed over the Upper Keys. The storm cost the lives of hundreds of people.

The weather bureau report at 10:00 p.m. in Key West on September 2 stated the temperature at 81 degrees and the winds out of the northwest at 34 miles per hour. "Hurricane warnings north of Everglades to Punta Gorda. Tropical disturbance of full hurricane intensity but rather small diameter central 8 pm near Matecumbe Key moving northwestward accompanied by shifting gales and hurricane winds near center." By the time the sun came up the next morning, the community of Islamorada had been effectively scrubbed clean from Upper Matecumbe. The Hotel Matecumbe was one of a handful of structures partially standing when the storm was over. The proprietors, Ed and Fern Butters, survived the storm. The hotel was later torn down.

Coconut palms were snapped in half and buildings were blown completely from their foundations, destroyed, and left in piles of debris. While the storm battered the islands from Key Largo to Vaca Key, the tightly wound hurricane centered its violence on the Upper Keys, the Matecumbe Keys in particular. The Caribbee Colony property was wiped off the beachfront (above); its manager, J.W. Dumas, was a casualty of the storm. The Matecumbe Club was leveled by wind gusts (below), reported to have approached 200 miles per hour, and by an estimated storm surge of 17 feet. In total, approximately 500 deaths were attributed to the storm, although the exact number will never be known.

The 1935 census counted 673 civilians living in the Upper Keys. Several hundred veterans represented the workforce stationed in Islamorada to build bridges. On Friday, August 30, 1935, 684 veterans showed up at the office to get paid. After getting paid, several hundred traveled to Key West or Miami to celebrate the Labor Day holiday. Hundreds remained in Islamorada. When the hurricane alarm was finally sounded to evacuate the area, a relief train was sent from Miami. After lunch on Monday, September 2, workers began preparing locomotive No. 447 for the run to the Keys. The train departed at 4:30 p.m. and arrived at the Islamorada depot just after 8:00 p.m. Meanwhile, the storm was delivering its blows. A 17-foot tidal surge washed the train from the track. The locomotive remained upright.

The tents and wooden shacks that formed the veterans' work camps stood no chance against the fury of the Category 5 hurricane. Hundreds of veterans died in the storm. Fortunately, the killer storm struck on a holiday weekend, when an estimated 300 veterans had gone to Key West and Miami to celebrate Labor Day. In addition, 11 veterans were reported to have stolen a truck and driven north to see the president. Like most everything else, the ferry landing was destroyed. Scores of miles of railroad tracks were ruined, and the devastation reshaped the area in other ways. Before the storm, a sandy beach area up to eight feet wide had built up along the Atlantic coastline. The storm redistributed the sand, leaving the area relatively free of natural sand beaches.

The top photograph shows what was left of the Lower Matecumbe ferry landing after the storm. Bridges linking Lower and Upper Matecumbe were destroyed by the hurricane. In order to facilitate automobile traffic between Key West and the mainland, a temporary ferry landing was constructed at the southern tip of Upper Matecumbe. That landing is shown below. The hurricane destroyed 40 miles of railroad tracks, but it was not just the hurricane that stopped the Flagler train from ever making the run to Key West again. The railroad had declared bankruptcy in 1932; the hurricane was just the nail in the coffin. The railroad right-of-way was sold to the state for $640,000. Because many of the railroad's concrete and steel bridges weathered the storm relatively intact, the decision was made to convert the railroad bridges to accommodate automobile traffic. The job of connecting the mainland and Key West with a continuous framework of roadways and bridges was completed in 1938.

As a result of the storm, bodies were washed across Florida Bay; one mother was found with her child 40 miles away. Some years after the Great Labor Day Hurricane of 1935, a car similar to one of these was discovered during a dredging project. Inside the vehicle were two skeletons; their deaths were attributed to the hurricane.

The initial death toll from the hurricane was listed at 423 people. There were other casualties associated with the storm, including bodies washed out into the Atlantic or into the backcountry that became tangled in the mangroves and picked apart by sharks, crabs, or buzzards. Later, 62 additional deaths were attributed to the storm, making the total 485 (228 civilians and 257 veterans).

The hurricane effectively cut off all communication to the Islamorada area, as well as any access on or off Islamorada. The above photograph shows the northern tip of Windley Key, where headquarters for the relief operation were established. The wooden highway and railroad bridges were destroyed in the hurricane. The railroad's concrete abutments were left intact. To reach Windley Key, a temporary walking bridge was rigged across the railroad bridge using cables and wooden planks, as seen at right.

When he moved from Rock Harbor, Berlin Felton built the original structure at this iconic spot in the early 1930s. Rumor suggests it was built to sell hard drinks during Prohibition. When O.D. King bought the property, it became known as King's Filling Station as well as the Rustic Inn. The gas station faced the Old Highway. After the storm, the site became home to Sid and Roxie's Green Turtle Inn.

As a result of the hurricane, on September 6, four days after the storm, Florida governor David Scholtz ordered the cremation of the victims' bodies to help prevent pestilence. The smell of the bodies had begun to fill the air, and relief workers were encouraged to use gas masks. Antiseptic practices were strictly enforced to prevent the spread of disease.

The *Sunday Tribune–Miami Beach*, dated September 8, 1935, stated that victims of the storm were awaiting transfer to the Miami Woodlawn Cemetery. The federal government paid $100 per body to handle the remains of each of the veterans. In this image, taken at the Snake Creek relief center, stacks of coffins are being loaded onto a barge for shipment to Miami.

Woodlawn Cemetery, on Southwest Eighth Street in Miami, was unable to handle all of the bodies, but 109 World War I veterans were buried there. After arrival from Islamorada, the bodies of the veterans were transferred from wooden coffins to copper-lined caskets that were then soldered shut by the undertaker. The caskets were then lowered into mass graves and covered by American flags.

The aftermath of the hurricane left a devastated Islamorada with little food, shelter, or fresh water. The only thing there was plenty of was bodies, hundreds of bodies. The air buzzed with flies and began to stink of death. Because every resource was overwhelmed, the governor ordered funeral pyres arranged and the bodies cremated. Pyres were constructed with wooden coffins, stacked one atop another, which were then doused with diesel fuel and set aflame. Burning ceremonies were overseen by a rabbi, priest, Protestant minister, civilian officials, and National Guardsmen. The ceremony was accompanied by a bugler playing "Taps" and a rifle salute. Several pyre sites were arranged in Islamorada. This funeral pyre was set on the Plantation Key bank of Snake Creek.

On September 7, 1935, Ernest Hemingway (pictured) wrote a letter to his editor and friend, Maxwell Perkins: "We were the first in to Camp Five of the veterans who were working on the Highway construction. Out of 187, only 8 survived. Saw more dead than I'd seen in one place since the Lower Piave in June of 1918." He also made this general note: "we made five trips with provisions for survivors to different places, but nothing but dead men to eat the grub. Max, you can't imagine it, two women, naked, tossed up into trees by the water, swollen and stinking, their breasts as big as balloons, flies between their legs . . . recognize them as the two very nice girls who ran a sandwich place and filling-station three miles from the ferry."

While the death and destruction wrought by the killer hurricane have been reported over and over, there are hundreds of stories from those who survived. The *Miami Tribune*, dated September 8, 1935, reported that Egan A. Taylor, a 68-year-old fisherman, "weathered the storm by clinging to the mast of his boat."

Leo Johnson lived on De Leon Avenue. His home was one of the few structures still standing after the hurricane crossed Islamorada. A theory as to why his home survived is that the toppled train cars acted as a sort of buffer against the wind and tide. Johnson, a local fishing guide, is seen here at right, at his house, with Ralph Gilespie.

The afternoon before the hurricane struck, Alonzo Cothron secured his property. He nailed his pet pig up in a crate for safekeeping. An article published by the *Miami Herald* reported that he left his flock of 20 ducks free, "thinking they would seek shelter under the house." Cothron returned to the Keys on Sunday, September 8, to find his house gone. His property was strewn with the "wreckage of roots and palm trees and then my pig pushed his nose out of a hole he had dug himself into, and came up running to me just like a dog." Of his ducks, 11 survived by seeking refuge in the hammock, emerging from the "jungle debris after the National Guard established a post at what remained of Islamorada." Since little fresh water was available, they appeared "very thirsty."

Those wishing to escape the horrors left by the storm and those relief workers trying to lend a hand were both caught in an automobile quagmire when they attempted to reach the Keys. This photograph, looking north of Snake Creek, shows the lines of cars stuck on Plantation Key.

As many as 15 burial sites were arranged around Islamorada to accommodate the ashes of the bodies burned in the assorted funeral pyres. This site was located across the street from what was once the Caribbee Colony resort property, across the road from what would likely be La Siesta Resort property today.

To deal with the horrific number of bodies, as many as 15 burial sites were arranged between the southern tip of Plantation Key and the southern tip of Lower Matecumbe, where the remains of the veterans' work camps had once stood. The monument shown below was referred to as Cremation Site No. 2. The remains of 44 cremated bodies were buried here. The marker is located on Upper Matecumbe, overlooking the Florida Bay, near mile marker 82. During the hurricane, members of the Russell family took refuge in a lime packinghouse near here.

Shown here is the construction of what would become known as the Florida Keys Memorial. The building directly behind the monument is the parsonage housing for the Matecumbe Methodist Church. The edge of the roof of the church can be seen behind the parsonage. The Harvey W. Seeds Post of the American Legion helped raise funds to build the monument, which was unveiled on November 14, 1937.

Seen here at the base of the covered monument is a small coffin wrapped in an American flag. At 1:00 p.m., burial services were conducted by Chaplin E.R. Reedy of the Henry Seeds Post, American Legion. The small casket contained the remains of Herman Saulter, a World War I veteran from Philadelphia whose remains were identified because his official discharge papers were found tucked inside his coat pocket.

Artist John Klinkenberg inscribed the bronze plaque below the monument's sculpture: "Dedicated To The Memory Of The Civilians And The War Veterans Whose Lives Were Lost In The Hurricane Of September Second 1935." Faye Marie Parker, nine years old in 1937, was one of the hurricane's survivors. She was invited to pull the cord that unveiled the Florida Keys Memorial. She was helped by two Boy Scouts.

The event was attended by as many as 4,000 people, including state dignitaries and practically every mayor from Key West to Fort Lauderdale. The 18-foot-tall obelisk represents the approximate height of the tidal surge that swept across the island. At the foot of the monument is a crypt in which ashes from the mass burial sites were interred. The Florida Keys Memorial is located at approximately mile marker 82.

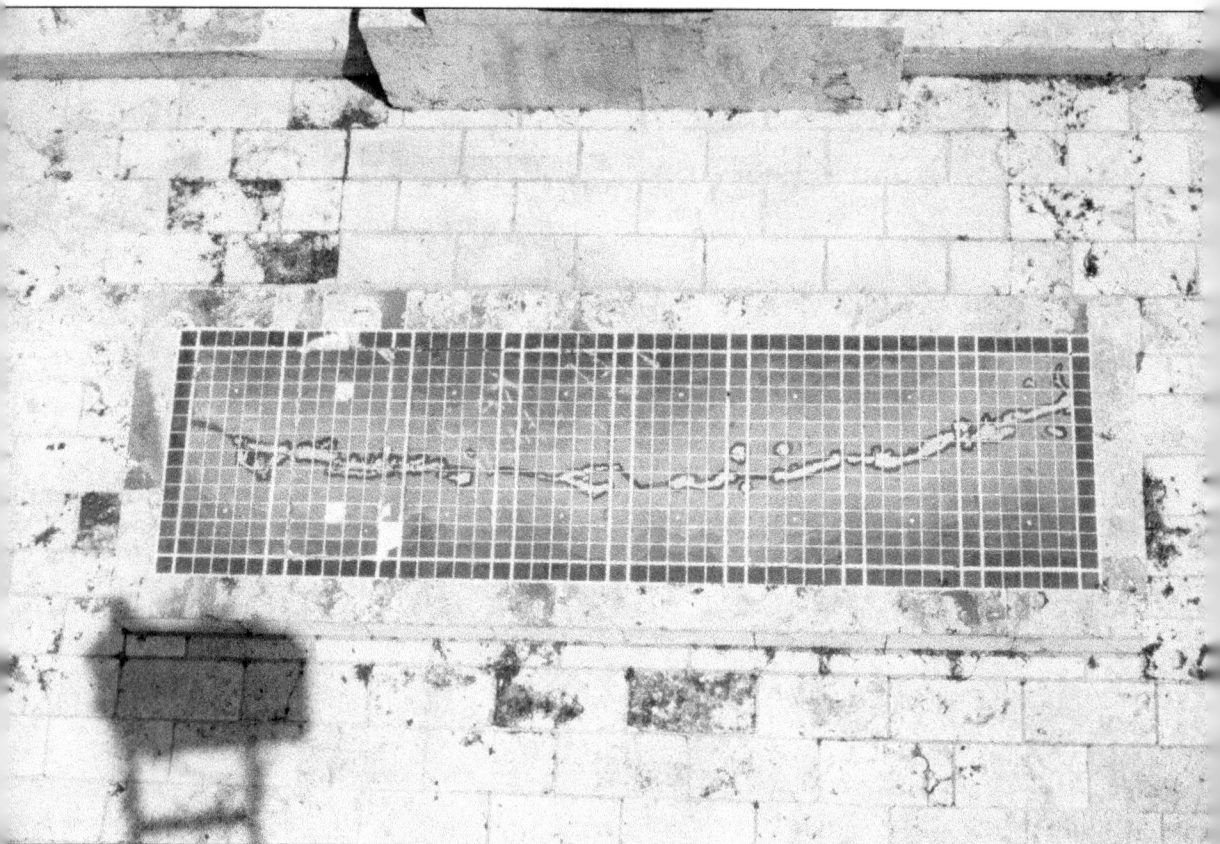

The crypt at the base of the monument is 22 feet long and filled with the remains of an undetermined number of victims of the 1935 hurricane. The exact number of bodies interred is difficult to determine because, two years after the caskets were stacked, burned, and buried in a minimum of three sites, ashes were dug back up and placed inside the newly modeled crypt. The mosaic tile work adorning the crypt was designed by Adela Gisbet and represents the span of islands, from Key Largo to Marathon, impacted by the Labor Day Hurricane. The last man interred inside the crypt was county commissioner Harry Harris, who died in 1978. After a brief period, Harris's remains were removed and reburied at their present site at Harry Harris Park in Tavernier.

Five

RECONSTRUCTION

After the Great Labor Day Hurricane of 1935, the community of Islamorada had to start rebuilding, from scratch. Except for one home, the churches, post office, and school were destroyed. This is what remained of the post office, the foundation of which can still be seen at the intersection of De Leon Avenue and the Old Highway. Brothers John and Clifton Russell had been sharing the duties of postmaster at the time of the storm.

By 1940, this building was the Over-Seas Inn. Before the storm, Willard and Eddie Sweeting, father and son, operated a grocery store at the location. The two-story wooden structure, one of the first rebuilt after the storm, was completed with the assistance of FERA and the Red Cross, who supplied the materials, but not the manpower. Finished in 1936, it served as the temporary school while the new school was being constructed on the other side of the highway. Classes were held downstairs and taught by Ferran Pinder. Rent for the room was $8.40 a month. The building was used for the 1936 and 1937 school years. Because more families had returned to the area, the downstairs and a room upstairs were rented for $40 per month. Today, it is home to Island Villa Properties, 81681 Old Highway.

Ferran Pinder (left) stands in front of the new storm refuge school constructed in response to the hurricane. Before the storm, Pinder taught at the two-room coral rock school, located on the beach at what is now the Cheeca Lodge property. During the course of the 1936 and 1937 school years, he taught at the temporary school located inside the Sweeting building. A teacher's wage in those days was approximately $75 per month.

In conjunction with President Roosevelt's Works Progress Administration and the Federal Emergency Relief Administration, the Red Cross helped with the construction of 33 buildings after the storm. The WPA was responsible for building the Islamorada and Tavernier schools, as well as the monument. The Red Cross and FERA built "hurricane houses," single-family homes for displaced residents. This FERA truck is being loaded with materials at a temporary concrete plant.

On January 2, 1936, four months to the day after the catastrophe, a Key West newspaper published a story discussing a series of proposed storm structures to be built: "hurricane proof community houses along the lower east coast and in the Lake Okeechobee and the keys region. The building will be of sufficient size to house the entire population in the area served by each. They will be used for school, church and general civic purposes and during the hurricane season will be used as houses of refuge in which people of the area may escape the dangers of high wind and water." In the Upper Keys, two buildings were constructed, one in Islamorada and one in Tavernier. The identical structures were built with 12-inch concrete walls reinforced with rebar to withstand the force of a major hurricane.

To help protect against storm surge, nearly all of the structures built by FERA and the WPA were erected on elevated foundations of 18-inch-thick poured concrete. Walls were constructed 12 inches thick and reinforced with rebar. Additionally, cisterns were built into the foundations to provide enough fresh water to last a small family through the dry season. The houses were built for free, providing the family owned the property the house was being built on.

Classes from the Sweeting building moved to their permanent residence across the street in September 1938. The Sweeting building became known as the Over-Seas Inn. Today, it is known as the Island Villa building, at 81681 Old Highway. The Matecumbe School across the highway closed its doors to students in 1951. The building has housed the Islamorada Branch of the Monroe County Library since 1966.

Because of how they were constructed, many of the Red Cross or hurricane houses can still be seen in the Upper Keys. A handful of the structures are visible while driving along the Oversea Highway on Upper Matecumbe. During the community's reconstruction period, Roy Wingate was sent to monitor the progress of the Keys Building Program. In a note regarding construction of the hurricane-proof structures, typed on March 3, 1936, Wingate writes to his superiors in Miami: "These buildings are as near wind and water proof as could be constructed. Cleverly designed and are being constructed as well as it is humanly possible to do so. The writer, since inspecting this project, feels that the Red Cross will have reason to feel proud of its part in this undertaking in the years to come."

A total of 27 concrete hurricane houses were built in Islamorada. A series of them were constructed along the oceanside of Upper Matecumbe, just south of the northern tip where the Russells first homesteaded the island. These houses were built for the surviving members of the Russell family. Another hurricane house, at 81120 Old Highway, was originally built for Everett and Dorothy Carey. Everett was the son of James Edwin and Clara (Thompson) Carey.

The Farm Security Administration (FSA), established in 1937, provided assistance to the rural poor and to migrant agricultural workers. The FSA also funded a photography unit, headed by Roy Stryker, to create a pictorial record of America. One of Stryker's agents, Arthur Rothstein, was the only photographer to come to the Keys, arriving in 1937. Seen here is the school foundation. (Courtesy Arthur Rothstein, Library of Congress, FSA-OWI Collection.)

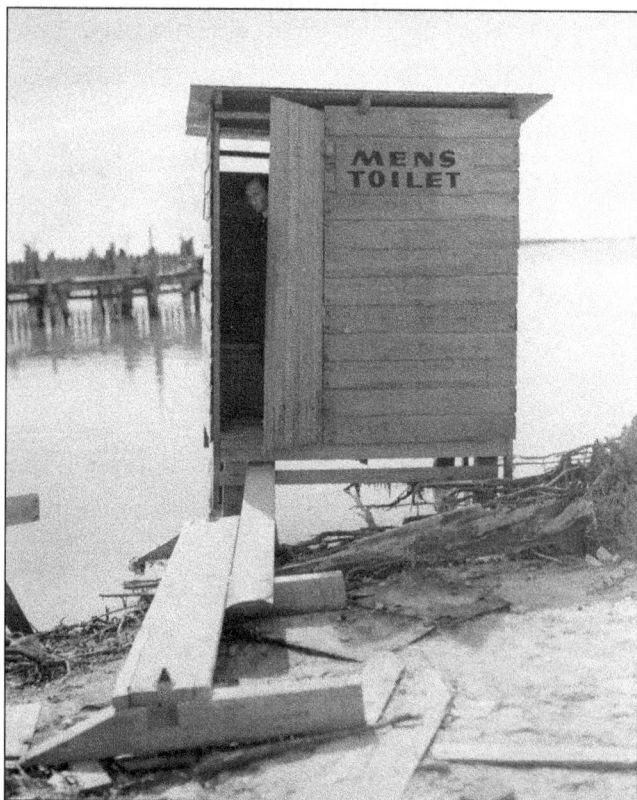

The Farm Security Administration's Arthur Rothstein was employed to photograph America. Rothstein's daughter, Annie, reports that her father "went everywhere, saw everything, and took a camera." He visited the Keys in 1937, stopping in Islamorada to take these two photographs, both on Lower Matecumbe. The photograph at left shows the men's toilet, which would have had a hole cut in the floor under the toilet seat. The changing tides would have flushed the waste away. In the above photograph, the fishermen's nets can be seen drying in the background. (Courtesy Arthur Rothstein, Library of Congress, FSA-OWI Collection.)

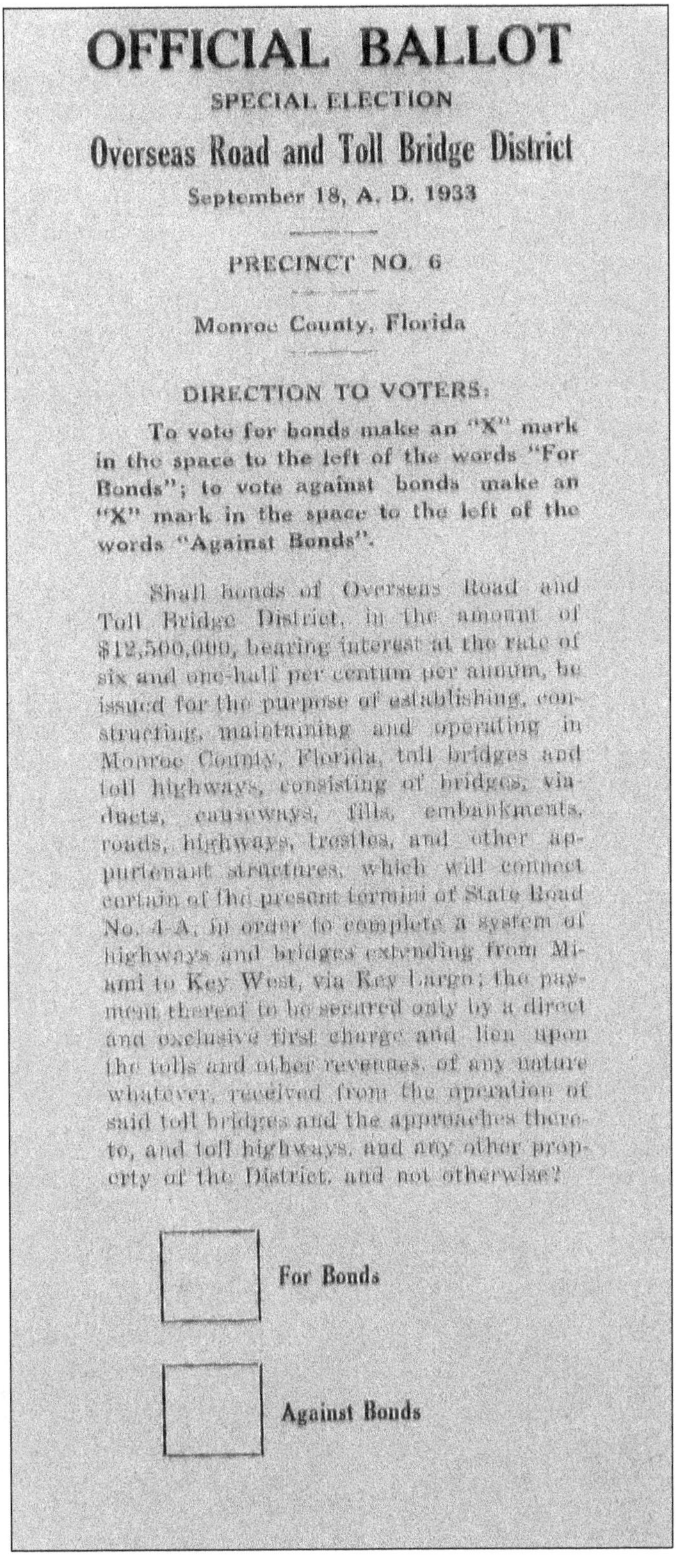

OFFICIAL BALLOT

SPECIAL ELECTION

Overseas Road and Toll Bridge District

September 18, A. D. 1933

PRECINCT NO. 6

Monroe County, Florida

DIRECTION TO VOTERS:

To vote for bonds make an "X" mark in the space to the left of the words "For Bonds"; to vote against bonds make an "X" mark in the space to the left of the words "Against Bonds".

Shall bonds of Overseas Road and Toll Bridge District, in the amount of $12,500,000, bearing interest at the rate of six and one-half per centum per annum, be issued for the purpose of establishing, constructing, maintaining and operating in Monroe County, Florida, toll bridges and toll highways, consisting of bridges, viaducts, causeways, fills, embankments, roads, highways, trestles, and other appurtenant structures, which will connect certain of the present termini of State Road No. 4-A, in order to complete a system of highways and bridges extending from Miami to Key West, via Key Largo; the payment thereof to be secured only by a direct and exclusive first charge and lien upon the tolls and other revenues, of any nature whatever, received from the operation of said toll bridges and the approaches thereto, and toll highways, and any other property of the District, and not otherwise?

☐ **For Bonds**

☐ **Against Bonds**

This special election ballot reads: "Shall bonds of Oversea Road and Toll Bridge District, in the amount of $12,500,000 bearing interest at the rate of six and one-half percent annum, be issued for the purpose of establishing, constructing, maintaining and operating in Monroe County, Florida, toll booth and toll highways, consisting of bridges, viaducts, causeways, fills, embankments, roads, highways, trestles and other appurtenant structures, which connect certain of the present termini of State Road No. 4-A, in order to complete a system of highways and bridges extending from Miami to Key West, via Key Largo; the payment thereof to be secured only by a direct and exclusive first charge and lien upon the tolls and other revenues, of any nature whatever, received from the operation of said toll bridges and the approaches there-to, and toll highways, and other properties of the District, and not otherwise?" (Courtesy Scott DeWolfe.)

While Flagler's bridges were being retooled to accommodate automobile traffic, it was still necessary to use the ferry. Shown here is a passenger ticket issued for passage on the ferry in 1937. The 15-foot vehicle had Maryland license plates. The system of bridges constructed to replace the ferry was completed in 1938. (Courtesy Scott DeWolfe.)

Alonzo Cothron and Berlin Felton were early business partners with holdings from Tavernier to Key West. A&B Lobster House is still named for Alonzo and Berlin. Felton's wife, Edith (left), poses with the legendary early Upper Keys guide Bonnie Smith and a rack of bonefish. The A&B Docks, where the ladies are posing, were once located on the bayside, where Morada Bay and Pierre's restaurants operate today.

Benjamin Lee Pinder stands on the A&B docks in front of two bonefish hanging from the rack. Born in 1878, he was the son of the original Pinder patriarch, Adolphus. Benjamin, the brother of the aforementioned Preston Pinder, married Marion Yulee on August 20, 1903. Ferran Pinder was his son, and Florence, his daughter. Benjamin died in 1940 and is buried beside his wife in the Pioneer Cemetery.

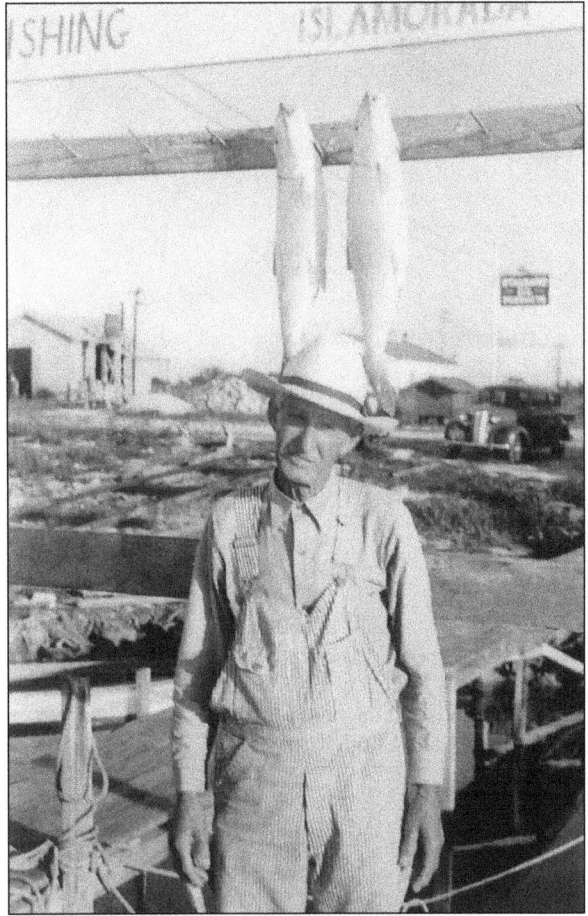

The Smith-Richardson house was built by Alonzo Cothron in 1937 or 1938. The Richardson family, heirs to the Vicks Chemical Company, commissioned Cothron to build an exclusive residence on the beach of Upper Matecumbe, near the site of the school and church destroyed by the 1935 hurricane. The property was later sold, first to the Stratton family and then to Al Mills, who named it Casa Islamorado.

The Casa Islamorado, owned by Albert J. Mills, opened in 1949 and was home to a hotel, restaurant, and bar. Clara May Downey, owner of the Olney Inn, in Olney, Maryland, purchased the property. Downy added 22 beachside bungalows nestled in a grove of 300 palm trees. She renamed the luxury resort the Olney Inn. One of Downey's first guests was Pres. Harry Truman.

Carl and Cynthia Twitchell, heirs to the A&P grocery chain, were the next to purchase the property. They changed the name from the Olney Inn to the Cheeca Lodge. "Cheeca" is a combination of Cynthia's nickname, Chee, and Carl. They refurbished the property, adding the main lodge, tennis courts, and golf course.

This photograph was taken on June 28, 1938, by someone standing near the hurricane monument and looking south along the Old Highway. The building on the left belonged to Capt. Ed Albury. The small sign in front of the building advertises "Sport Fishing Year Round." Kaiyo Restaurant operates on that property today. The tall square building is Sweeting's Over-Seas Inn, known as the Island Villa property today. Where Chef Michael's stands today, there was a gas station with two pumps. On a sign not visible without a magnifying glass, posted near the gas station, a Florida Ticket Office is advertised. It is possible that this is where automobile drivers wishing to go beyond Lower Matecumbe Key purchased tickets for the ferry ride to No Name Key.

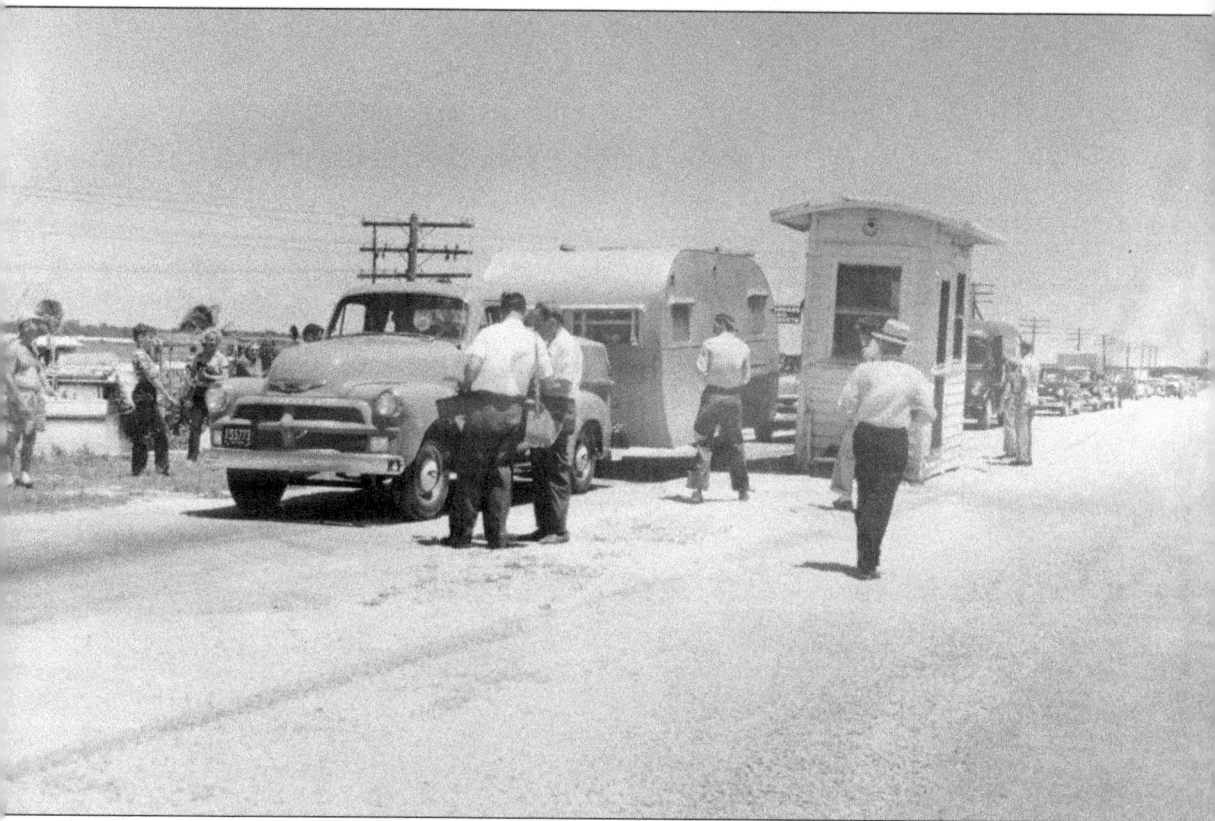

The rebuilt Oversea Highway opened to traffic on March 29, 1938. The official, celebrated opening took place on July 4, 1938. Pres. Franklin Roosevelt was driven to Key West along the highway in an open convertible on February 18, 1939. He then boarded the Navy cruiser *Houston* to watch war games in the Caribbean. To help recoup costs associated with completing the solid bridge system linking Lower Matecumbe to the rerouted end of the highway at Big Pine Key, a toll of $1 per vehicle, including the driver, was charged. Passengers were assessed a fee of 25¢ each. Beginning on January 1, 1953, Monroe County residents were given a free pass. In April of the following year, all tolls were lifted and the booths removed. Lower Matecumbe's Toll Gate Inn is visible in the background of this c. 1940 photograph.

The pier stretches out from what is now the Moorings property. Sprouting coconut trees can be seen repopulating the beach where mature trees stood before the storm. Several hurricane houses are visible, as is the Over-Seas Inn and the hurricane monument in the top right quadrant of the photograph. To get an idea of where the highway is, the hurricane monument stands between the old road and new highways. This is the general area of Upper Matecumbe, where the Pinders homesteaded. This 1940s photograph reveals how the community had rebounded after the 1935 hurricane. It also shows how the community of Islamorada began redeveloping. Both the commercial and sport fishing industries began to expand in the 1940s. Visitors needed hotels and restaurants and fishing guides.

"PETE" und "REPEAT"   THEATER OF THE SEA - 73 MILES SOUTH OF MI.

The water feature at Theater of the Sea is a former quarry dug by Flagler's men. Before it was where dolphins were taught tricks, it was used to raise stone crabs by Alonzo Cothron and Berlin Felton, the quarry's owners. Phelps McKenny leased and made Theater of the Sea what it is today. While vacationing from his native Georgia, McKenny saw the property's water feature and imagined dolphins jumping out from the water, splashing and leaping to the delight of audiences. Theater of the Sea opened in 1946. Its first performing Atlantic bottle-nosed dolphin was trained and delivered by Grassy Key's Milton Santini, the man who trained the television and movie star Flipper. Theater of the Sea is the second-oldest marine mammal park in the world. It was the third marine mammal facility in the United States to offer a swim-with-the-dolphins experience.

These two men were stalwarts of the community and survivors of the Great Labor Day Hurricane of 1935. Their descendents are still prominent members of the community. The man on the left is Preston Pinder, grandson of Richard Pinder, who was farming bananas on Indian Key in 1870. Preston Street, found on Upper Matecumbe Key, is named after Preston Pinder. John A. Russell (right) lost his wife, three children, and a grandchild to the Great Labor Day Hurricane of 1935. His father sold William J. Krome the original 15 acres of Upper Matecumbe, which Krome named Isla Morada in 1907.

Howard G. Whidby arrived in the Upper Keys with the Coast Guard. He married his wife, Ethel, and opened Whimpy's Place just north of Theater of the Sea. Whimpy, as he was known, shrimped with his wife at night in Tavernier Creek. They kept the shrimp alive in traps at the end of the small pier behind the shack. Here, Howard and Ethel pose in front of the shack.

Another shack on Windley Key was the Green Mangrove Restaurant. In 1952, Ed Goebel purchased the restaurant, along with the 7-Mile Reef Marina and five rental units. Goebel renamed the restaurant the Big Blow. It is seen here around 1947. He also bought the ocean floor around the property as well as a dredge. Goebel developed what would become the Holiday Isle property, called the Post Card Inn today.

The Green Turtle Inn replaced the Rustic Inn. According to the *Florida Weekly News* of October 25, 1947, "Sid and Roxy Siderius who previously operated the Seabreeze Bar and Restaurant will have the formal opening of the Green Turtle Inn at Islamorada, Saturday, October 25th. Free drinks and eats from 7 to 9. The public is cordially invited." The Green Turtle's menu featured turtle steaks, soups, and chowders. Sid and Roxy also operated a fish house and turtle cannery up the highway on the bay side of the island. The cannery had wooden pens along the shores, called turtle kraals, where live turtles were kept. A few rental units were located next to the restaurant where visitors and fishermen could spend the night.

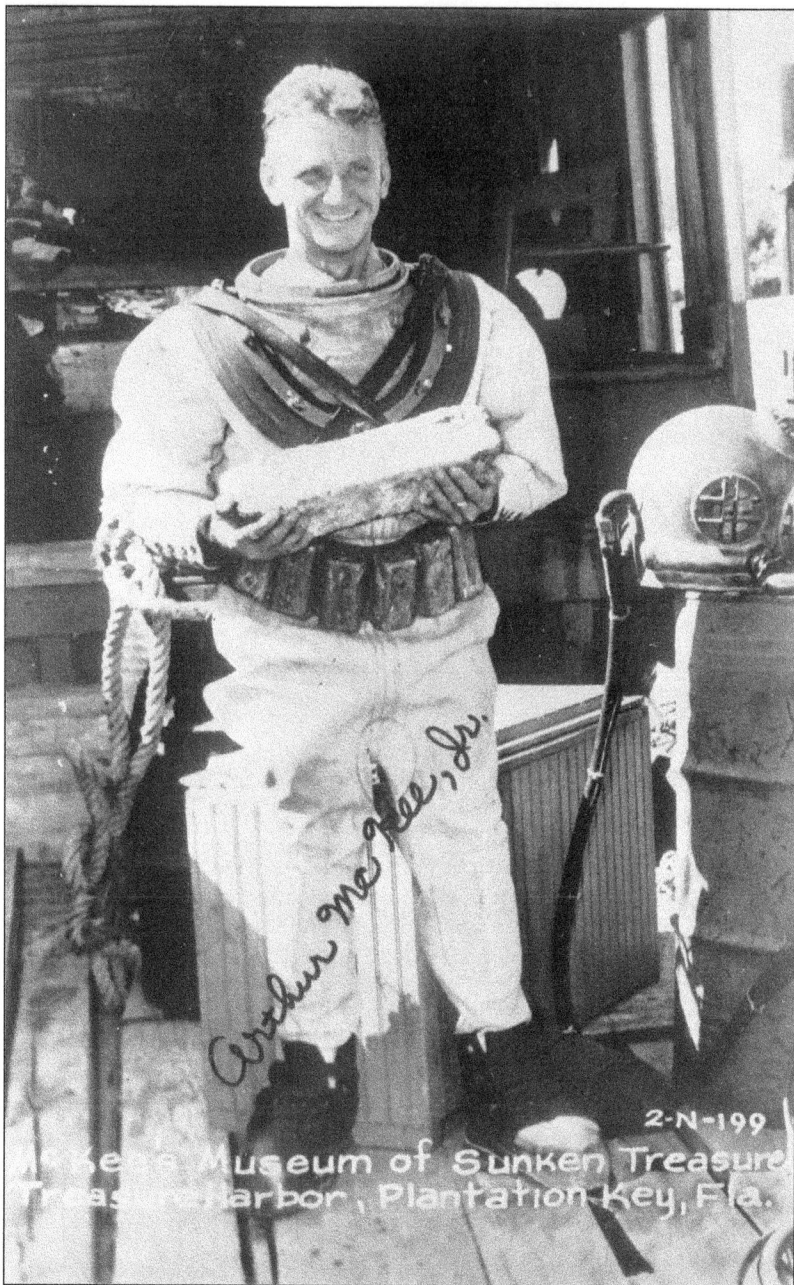

McKee's Museum of Sunken Treasure
Treasure Harbor, Plantation Key, Fla.

2-N-199

Before Key West had Mel Fisher, Islamorada had Arthur "Silver Bar" McKee Jr., born November 2, 1910, in Bridgeton, New Jersey. He spent time as a lifeguard and served an apprenticeship with a hard-hat diver as a line tender before moving to Homestead in 1937. He bought a used hard-hat diving rig in Miami and found work on the Navy's 18-inch water pipeline project running from Homestead to Key West. McKee also inspected bridge piers. Life changed for McKee after the Windley Key fishing guide, Reggie Roberts, showed McKee the remains of a warship that had escorted the doomed 1733 Spanish Treasure Fleet. He began acquiring Spanish archival maps. While working with Charles Brookfield on a treasure expedition in the Bahamas, McKee found three silver bars of 60, 70, and 75 pounds. "Silver Bar" McKee died in 1980.

McKee incorporated his Museum of Sunken Treasure, selling 20,000 shares for $10 apiece. Charles Brookfield was the museum's vice president. The first museum, operating from 1948 to 1952, was built at what today is Treasure Harbor Marina. A small sign placed along the highway had an arrow and the words "Spanish Treasure." This second, larger museum, built by Alonzo Cothron with a treasure vault, is today found across the highway from Betsy the lobster.

This 1950 aerial photograph of Upper Matecumbe shows a growing community. South of the hurricane monument is Capt. Ed Albury's home and the Sweeting building. The cluster of buildings closest to Florida Bay is located near where the Morada Bay and Pierre's restaurants stand today. In 1950, this was home to the A&B docks, a grocery store, a bait and icehouse, and a machine shop.

In 1948, PTA president Katherine "K" Wilkinson spearheaded the effort to petition the Monroe County School Board for a high school in the Upper Keys. Prior to this, the only high school was located in Key West. In response, the school board obtained 16 acres of land from Mrs. P.L. Wilson for $5,800. The Coral Shores School opened in 1951 with six classrooms and six teachers for grades first through eleventh. Charles Albury, referred to as "Prof." Albury, was the principal, and Ferran Pinder was his assistant. In 1952, twelfth grade was added and the school was formally dedicated. Students from Marathon were brought to Greyhound Key (Fiesta Key) and shuttled by bus to the school. The first graduating class accepted their diplomas on June 10, 1953. "Prof." Albury (left) retired in 1965.

SNAKE CREEK FISHING LODGE — 72 MILES SOUTH OF MIAMI, FLORIDA
RESTAURANT — BAR — COTTAGES — CHARTER BOATS

In *The Miami News* of November 25, 1949, "Salty Says" columnist Salty Mallants reported, "The joint was jumping the other eve when Elwood Dillin again opened his Snake Creek Lodge. It seems the entire population of the Keys was in on the doings and many out of state tourists decided to stop in and get in on the fun. Dillin is an old timer on the Florida Keys. He intends to again cater to his old customers and with that in mind he has engaged six skippers and their boats to operate out of his docks. After a shutdown of more than a year it is sort of welcome to see the lodge bathed in lights again. And he told this reporter he's going to put in skiffs while Bill Klys will take care of the bait situation."

PLANTATION YACHT HARBOR — "The Sportsman's Paradise" — 68 MILES SOUTH OF MIAMI — 100% AIR CONDITIONED CABINS — COCKTAIL LOUNGE, DINING ROOM, SWIMMING POOL, TENNIS COURTS, DANCING — Finest Fisherman's Resort in Florida —

According to the family of George Albury, George sold the property to a rich Cuban gambler from Key West in 1939, a man named Rend. It is said that Rend sold the property after World War II to Meyer Lansky, a notorious Mafia figure. Rumor suggests it was to be used as a gambling site. Today, the marina is part of Founders Park.

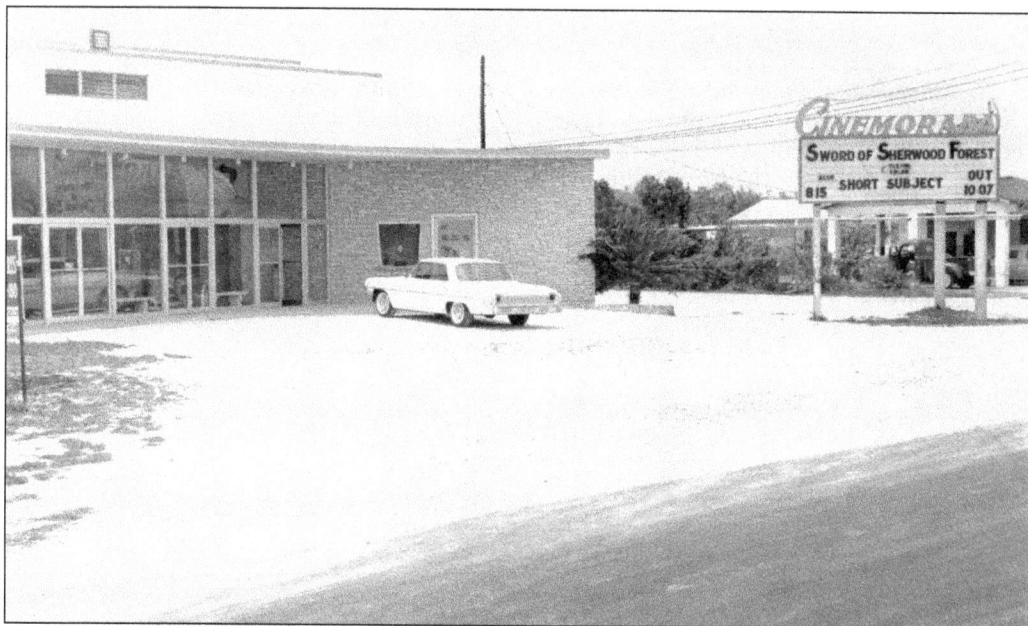

Home to Island Community Church today, this property was originally developed by Maj. Robert L. Duncan and his wife, who invested $120,000 building the Cinemorada Theatre. The 554-seat theater opened its doors around 1955 and was featured in *Boxoffice* magazine on December 7, 1957. The parking lot could accommodate 200 vehicles. According to the magazine, summer residency was approximately 5,000 in the Upper Keys, while winter residency spiked to approximately 17,000.

This photograph from the first annual Key Lime Festival in 1953 features, from left to right, Joanne Byrum, Key Largo Princess; Carolyn Smith, Islamorada Princess; Dorothy Albury, Islamorada Queen; Barbara "Babs" Kaufman, Islamorada Princess; and Jackie Sweeting, Islamorada Princess. The festival was aimed at attracting visitors to the Upper Keys. According to newspaper accounts, several thousand people attended, dined at a fish fry, and watched a parade of decorated yachts. Saluting the festival, a barrage of limes was fired from one of Art McKee's cannons.

It was 1952 when Ed Goebel bought a small restaurant on Windley Key, on a narrow strip of Atlantic front property. After purchasing several acres of seafloor, he brought in a dredge and began filling in the oceanfront property until he created seven additional acres, on which he created the Holiday Isle complex (now the Postcard Inn). These two photographs, taken from about the same viewpoint, show the development of the marina and the creation of the parking lot, still in use today. In the 1970s, what is now the World Famous Tiki Bar, birthplace of the rumrunner, was nothing more than a small wooden shack built out of driftwood, because, according to Goebel's son Greg, "money was tight."

On December 17, 1956, Horace Sutton wrote an article for *Sports Illustrated* titled "Footloose Sportsman." In it, he described the restaurant shown above, located on Indian Key Fill: "A few minutes to the south, on pilings sunk into the Gulf of Mexico, is Blueberry Hill Key, a restaurant domain of two white houses surrounded by a picket fence, connected to U.S. 1 by a small runway, and equipped with a red life preserver, presumably for diners who come a cropper returning to their cars. Dinner is by reservation only, your request being carried on telephone wires strung over the water." The restaurant was destroyed by Category 4 Hurricane Donna in 1960 (below).

In the late 1970s, many of the bridges linking the islands of the Keys were rebuilt. While only one drawbridge remains along the Oversea Highway, once upon a time several existed, including a state-run drawbridge at mile marker 78. Above, Upper Matecumbe can be seen in the distance. At the center of the image, a small building on stilts on the bay side of the highway was once the locale of Blackwell's Resort and then Blueberry Hill Restaurant. The small dock and building seen at the bottom of the top picture would later become part of Lower Matecumbe's Robbie's Marina. To the right of the roadway is the water pipeline. The bottom photograph is a close-up of the drawbridge that once stood near Mile Marker 78 between the Upper and Lower Matecumbe Keys.

Donna was a Category 4 hurricane that struck the Keys on September 10, 1960, with sustained winds of 140 miles per hour. Gusts were approximated at between 175 and 180 miles per hour. The eye of the storm crossed Duck Key at approximately mile marker 61. The Upper Keys were devastated and left without running water. The water pipeline was broken in five places, bridges were wrecked, and sections of roadway were washed out. The above photograph shows the southern tip of Upper Matecumbe. In the below photograph of a bridge taken out, the southern tip of Windley Key is visible.

August "Augie" and Helen Cockerham built a house behind their garage near mile marker 80.5. Then, six months later, Hurricane Donna raged across the Upper and Middle Keys during the middle of the night. During the storm, the Cockerhams' house was half-filled with seaweed, and the garage lost its roof. Their son Max went on to open Max's Marine on the other side of the highway.

Capt. Ed and Fern Butters moved away from Islamorada in 1935 after losing their Matecumbe Hotel in the 1935 hurricane. They moved to California before returning to Islamorada in the late 1940s. They operated the Fern Inn from 1950 to 1967 and were said to be living in one of the two buildings seen here when Hurricane Donna swept across the Keys.

The *Inagua Arrow*, a 150-foot tanker, attempted to navigate the Florida Straits during the hurricane. The tanker had taken on seawater for ballast, but the high winds and heavy swells pushed the vessel onto the property of Plantation Key resident Charles Dean. This photograph was taken by Fern Butters.

These are the remains of the Coral Grill after Donna blew the original wooden structure to pieces. When the restaurant was rebuilt, the Coral Grill was a single-story concrete building. In subsequent years, a second story was added. The restaurant offered an all-you-can-eat seafood buffet. In 1988, the cost was $13.95. As of 2013, the pink building is still standing; the sign is still there, too.

The storm was referred to in the news as "Deadly Donna." In the state of Florida, 12 deaths were attributed to the storm: six drownings, four heart attacks, one fatal car accident, and one electrocution. The tidal surge reached 12 feet in some areas. These photographs show damage wrought by Hurricane Donna to the Chesapeake Inn, which opened in the late 1950s. During the storm, six people sought refuge from the rising waters inside the tower, seen at left above. Today, the building and tower are part of the Whale Harbor property. The Chesapeake property is now just south of the Whale Harbor complex.

In the early 1950s, Clara May Downey had a houseboat towed in from Miami and pulled onto her Olney Inn property (now the Cheeca Lodge). She used the houseboat, *Bay Bourne*, as a rental unit. It is seen here nestled in a grove of coconut palms. Pres. Harry Truman and his wife, Bess, were guests in 1955 and 1957. Famed news anchor Edward R. Murrow was also a guest. During Hurricane Donna, the *Bay Bourne* was washed from this locale and pushed into the middle of Preston Street. Jim Gilmore, an Indianapolis 500 race car driver, bought the *Bay Bourne* from Downey. He added the second deck to the houseboat.

Capt. Angus Boatwright (above) built the second full-time residence on Lower Matecumbe Key. On Indian Key Fill, Boatwright operated his fish camp, offering rowboats for $1 a day (below). On Saturday, April 23, 1960, the captain departed for the Bahamas with his mate, Kent Hokanson, and four customers on a deep-sea fishing adventure aboard his ship *Muriel III*. Off of Cay Sal Bank, two Texas desperados who had run out of gas and were holed up at the lighthouse swam out and shot Boatwright, who later died. The "pirates" fled to Cuba, and the ship was returned to Boatwright's widow. The captain's shark rifle was also recovered, with a jammed bullet in the chamber.

Six

FISHING

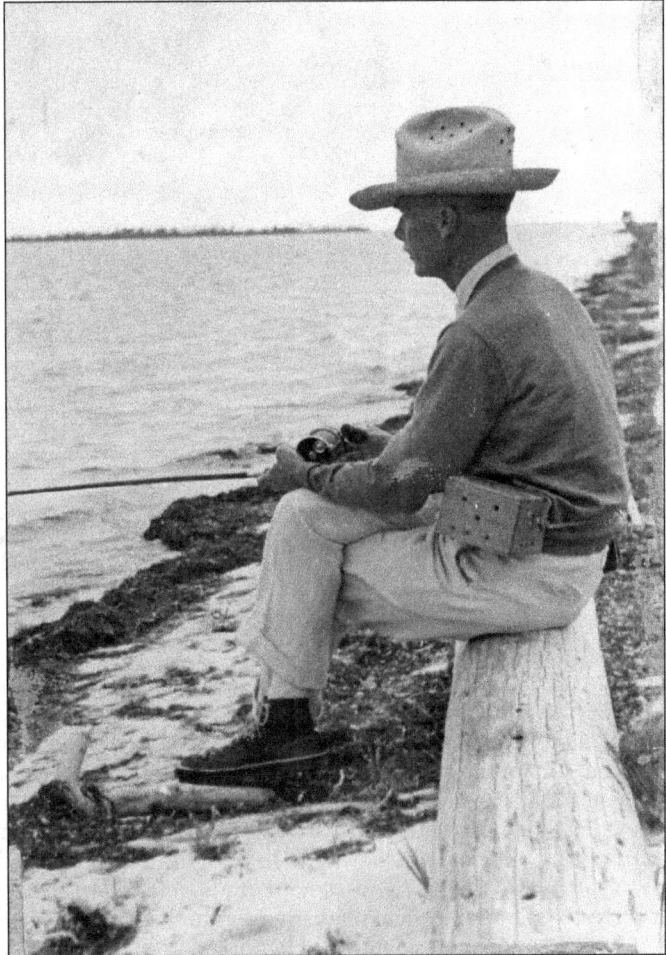

Pictures of men with fishing poles in their hands have been captured in the Florida Keys since cameras and fishing poles first coexisted. Here, Henry J. Howell sits on a driftwood log. According to accounts sworn to by John A. Russell, Islamorada's postmaster, in the year of the Great Labor Day Hurricane, Mr. Howell was a winter resident of Islamorada.

Ted Williams was an Islamorada fixture for over three decades. It was not uncommon to see the baseball great standing on a skiff, intently casting across a seagrass flat or into a backcountry channel. Two out of his three all-time favorite fish lived in the shallows surrounding the archipelago. Williams approached fishing the way he approached baseball, with serious intent, and he appreciated being left alone so he could focus. Sometimes he fished alone, and at other times he would go out with one of the local guides, Jimmie Albright, Gary Ellis, Jack Brothers, or any of a handful of others. While Williams frequented many, he referred to all other guides by the same name, Bush, a derivative of bush-league, referring to something amateurish in nature. Here, he is pictured at left with Islamorada resident Bill Hammond at the Islamorada Fishing Club.

Ev. Fowler's
CARIBEE YACHT BASIN
76 Miles South of Miami
ISLAMORADA, FLORIDA

After the 1935 hurricane, Ev and Suzie Fowler developed the deepwater lagoon found at the end of Upper Matecumbe into the Caribee Yacht Basin. In addition to a marina and restaurant (later known as Papa Joe's), a footbridge was constructed that crossed the lagoon to where nine cabins were built. In the early days, electricity was furnished with the help of a windmill. In the late 1930s and 1940s, Edney Parker ran a charter boat out of Fowler's for $50 a day. Also in the 1940s, Don Wollard ran the first airboat in the Keys out of Fowler's. He was also the Keys' distributor for Evinrude outboard motors. Another Parker, Norman, said that he met Shirley Temple when she stopped at the restaurant with her family to eat.

Jimmie Albright was considered one of the top fishing guides of his time and a pioneer and innovator in the field of fly fishing. He invented two knots indispensable to anglers, the nail knot and the Albright special. During his career, he fished with the likes of Jimmy Stewart, Ernest Hemingway, and Zane Grey. During leave from his service in the Navy, Albright visited Islamorada and booked a fishing charter with Capt. Bonnie Smith, who introduced Albright to the joy of bonefish as well as to her sister, Frankee. The two married after his return from World War II. His brother-in-law was the legendary Bill Smith, the first man to catch a bonefish and permit using a fly rod. Smith taught Albright everything he knew about Keys fishing. This is Albright aboard his boat, the *Rebel*.

Bud & Mary Stapleton
"original owners"
circa 1949

Though the ashes of Bud and Mary Stapleton have long since been scattered in local waters, their spirit and their names have remained an essential part of Islamorada history. Bud 'n' Mary's has been an icon in the Upper Keys since the mid-1940s. The Stapletons ventured south from New England, bought a piece of property on the southern tip of Upper Matecumbe Key, and opened a small hotel and tackle shop. It was after local captain Don Gurgiolo convinced them to let him build a small dock for his boat that the marina began to take shape. Both of these photographs are dated 1949. The above photograph shows Bud and Mary. At right, Bud is standing atop the carcass of a whale shark that floated in with the tide near the marina.

According to the Florida Keys Fishing Guides Association, Ted Williams, along with Pete and Lynette Siman and Don Hawley, came up with the ground rules and concept of scoring, conservation, and sportsmanship for the Islamorada Invitational Gold Cup Tarpon Tournament. It was a spin, plug, and fly tournament. Legendary guide Cecil Keith said, "the real reason Ted founded the tournament was to help the guides obtain business." In its inaugural year, Jake Muller guided Pete Siman to the championship. Ted Williams, guided by Jimmie Albright, caught the largest tarpon, at 96.5 pounds. Don Hawley, guided by George Hommell, caught seven fish, the most of the bunch. The contest was renamed the Islamorada Invitational Tarpon Fly Tournament. The year 2013 marks its 50th anniversary. Shown here are, from left to right, (first row) Jimmie Albright, Cecil Keith, Rolie Hollenbeck, and Jake Muller; (second row) Ted Williams, Lynette Siman, Jean Wolfe, and Pete Siman.

Here, four men pose with two tarpon. The man standing to the left is unidentified and likely a client of one of the three esteemed gentlemen to the right, Cecil Keith (center) and George Hommell. Jimmie Albright is kneeling in front. Keith was a protégé of Jimmie Albright, who learned his craft from the first man to ever catch a bonefish using a fly rod, Bill Smith. Keith would later help to develop and refine techniques used to catch sailfish while fly-fishing. In an article published by Vin T. Sparano on June 9, 2009, in *Sport Fishing Magazine*, Keith is quoted as saying, "In those days my boat was a 16-footer with a 5hp outboard motor. We never had to go far from the dock because bonefish (and likely tarpon) were everywhere."

Capt. Bill Smith and his wife, Bonnie, hold a special place in Florida Keys fishing history. In 1932, Captain Bill guided Ed and Fern Butters at the Matecumbe Hotel. Smith was not only the first man to document catching a bonefish on a fly-fishing rod, but was also the first to catch a permit in the same manner. In the summer of 1938, Smith caught his first bonefish on fly, but cheated, a little, by wrapping a hook with feathers and pork rind. To prove that he could land this fish on a legitimate fly, he spent months perfecting bonefish flies. Smith's wife, Bonnie, was also a guide as far back as the 1940s. During the war, she took a soldier named Jimmie Albright bone-fishing. Albright would later marry Bonnie's sister, Frankee, who was also a fishing guide.

In the late 1930s, Capt. Walter A. Starck and his son Walter E. "Buck" Starck bought what would later become the Whale Harbor Marina and Restaurant area. After World War II, the father and son sold the Whale Harbor property and ventured south, where they purchased the Lower Matecumbe property known today as Robbie's Marina. The building that is now home to the Hungry Tarpon Restaurant was originally used as a bait-and-tackle shop run by Buck Starck's wife, Ruth. Buck Starck ran his charter boat, WAS, out of the Lower Matecumbe marina. Pres. Harry S. Truman, who served in office from 1945 to 1953, is seen in the back of the WAS wearing the white hat. Edward R. Murrow is also on board. The WAS was retired in the mid-1970s.

As long as there have been bridges in the Florida Keys, there have been people fishing off them. This c. 1950 photograph shows a row of men and women fishing from the Whale Harbor Bridge. Windley Key is shown in the distance, before the Holiday Isle property had been developed. Note the fashionable shoes worn by the woman to the far right; she is wearing wedges.

Before it was Whale Harbor Marina and Restaurant, it was simply the Whale Harbor Fish Camp. In the late 1930s, Capt. Walter A. Starck and his son Walter E. "Buck" Starck developed the property that would include a bar, restaurant, service station, and several rental cottages. This photograph shows the marina in October 1957. The highway and bridge can be seen in the background.

In the early 1950s, Upper Keys fishing guides were the main impetus behind the development of the Islamorada Fishing Club. The first board of directors included Marin Dewey, Bill Knowles Sr., Bill Smith, Cecil Green, and Buck Starck. Guides associated with the club were largely responsible for creating the rules and regulations for fishing inside the boundaries of Everglades National Park. This building is home to the club today.

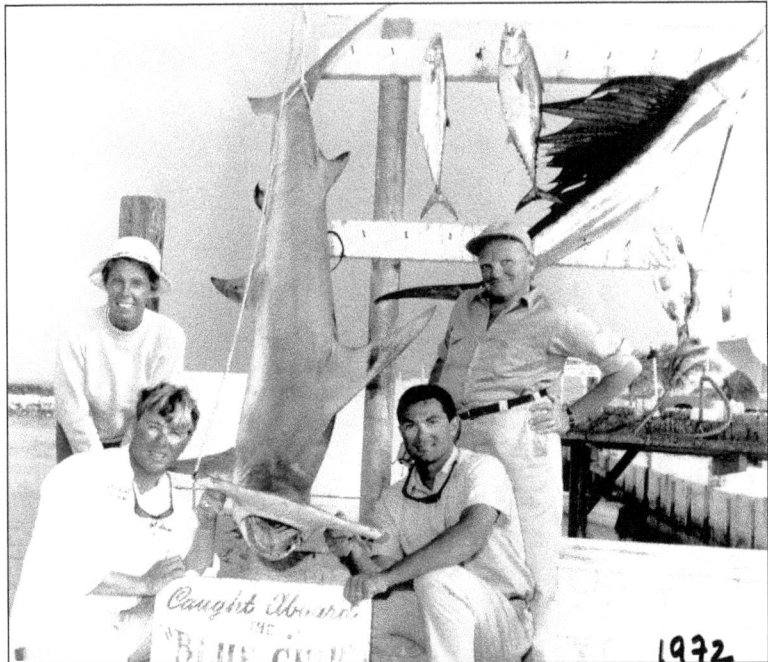

Capt. Skip Bradeen, pictured here at lower left, grew up working on the docks of his father's Long Island, New York, marina. Bradeen came for vacation in 1964 and never left. He worked as a deckhand on the Whale Harbor docks before establishing his storied career aboard his charter boat *Blue Chip*. His local claim to fame is the discovery of the "little Islamorada hump" in 340 feet of water.

Visit us at
arcadiapublishing.com

••

www.ingramcontent.com/pod-product-compliance
Lightning Source LLC
Chambersburg PA
CBHW050638110426
42813CB00007B/1845